S0-APM-414

THINKERS
THROUGH
TIME

THINKERS THROUGH TIME

Reading Ethics with Literature

by

Sister Mary Bernard Curran, O.P.

Bell Buckle, Tennessee

Library of Congress Cataloging-in-Publication Data

Curran, Mary Bernard, 1930-
Thinkers Through Time: reading ethics with literature/by Mary Bernard Curran.
p. cm.
Includes bibliographical references and index.
ISBN 0-916078-31-0
1. Ethics. 2. Literature and morals.   I. Title.
BJ1012.C86   1993   93-23843
170--dc20   CIP

Copyright Dominican Sisters - St. Cecilia Congregation, Nashville, TN.

No part of this book can be reproduced without the permission of Iris Press, Box 486, Bell Buckle, TN 37020.

The following publishers have generously given permission to use extended quotations from copyrighted works: From After Virtue by Alasdair MacIntyre. Copyright 1984 by the University of Notre Dame Press. From Nicomachean Ethics by Aristotle and translated by W.D. Ross. Copyright 1925 by Oxford University Press. From "Aristotle" by G.B. Kerford and from "Gabriel Marcel" by Samuel McMurray Keen. Copyright 1967 by Macmillan, Inc. Reprinted by permission of Macmillan Publishing Company from The Encyclopedia of Philosophy, Paul Edwards, Editor in Chief, Vols. 1 (p. 152) and 5 (p. 153), respectively. From Oedipus Rex of Sophocles: An English Version translated by Dudley Fitts and Robert Firtzgerald. Copyright 1949 by Harcourt Brace & Company and renewed in 1977 by Cornelia Fitts and Robert Fitzgerald. From Dictionary of Philosophy edited by Dagobert D. Runes. A Littlefield Adams Quality Paperback. Copyright 1983 by Rowan and Littlefield Publishers, Inc. From Critique of Practical Reason by Immanuel Kant and translated by Lewis White Beck. Copyright 1956 by Macmillan College Publishing Company, Inc. From Formalism in Ethics and Non-Formal Ethics of Values by Max Scheler and translated by Manfred S. Frings and Roger L. Funk. Copyright 1973 by Northwestern University Press. From The Second Coming by Walker Percy. Copyright 1980 by Farrar, Straus & Giroux. From Re-Reading Levinas by Robert Bernasconi and Simon Critchley. Copyright 1991 by Indiana University Press. From A History of Ancient Western Philosophy by Joseph Owens. Copyright 1959 by Prentice-Hall, Inc.

For my parents
Bernard H. Curran and Jean M. Curran

Acknowledgments

The following should be thanked: Mother Christine Born, O.P., Sister Rose Marie Masserano, O.P., Father Carl J. Hood, Mr. Robert Klyce, and Father William M. Nolan.

Contents

Acknowledgments   vii
Preface   xiii
Introduction   1
PART ONE
I   **Plato**   7
     Justice Is Useful
       Being Truthful and Paying Debts
       Benefiting Friends and Harming Enemies
       Advantage of the Stronger
       Tyranny, Injustice, Power
       Justice a Virtue
     On Sophocles' *Antigone*
II **Aristotle**   25
     Happiness is Virtuous
       Happiness as the Good
       Rationality as the Function of Man
       Virtue as Human Good
       Virtue as Pleasant to the Noble
       Happiness and Prosperity
       Rationality, Virtue, Durability
     On Sophocles' *Oedipus Rex*
III **St. Thomas Aquinas**   39
     Morality Is Reasonable
       Self-evident Principles
       The First Principle of Morality
       The Habit of Morality
       The Naturalness of Virtue
       The Universality of the Law
       The Unchangeableness of the Law
       The Law in the Heart
     On Dante's *Inferno*, canto v

IV **Immanuel Kant**   57
    Intention Is Decisive
        The Moral Law
        The Letter and the Spirit
        The Law of Duty
        Desires and Inclinations
        Moral Fanaticism
    On Henrik Ibsen's *The Wild Duck*
V   **Max Scheler**   82
    Person Is Primary
        A Wholly Sound Mind
        Soul-substance and Character
        Accountability and Responsibility
        Love of the Person
        A Certain Level of Development
        Domination over the Lived Body
    On Walker Percy's *The Second Coming*
VI **Gabriel Marcel**   97
    Communion Is Real
        Sanctity and Philosophy
        Intimacy, Availability, Presence
        Hope and Fidelity
        Mystery and Problem
        Function in the System
        The Ontological Need
    On Karol Wojtyla's *The Jeweler's Shop*
VII **Emmanuel Levinas**   115
    Transcendence Is Self-less
        The Other
        Subjectivity and Responsibility
        Passivity
        Vulnerability
        The Bond between the Subject and the Good
        Transcendence
    On Albert Camus's *The Plague*

VIII **Pope John Paul II**   127
  Mercy Is Divine
  The Father
  Christ
  The Old Testament
  The Prodigal Son
  Mother of Mercy
  On Shusaku Endo's "Mothers"

PART TWO
IX **St. Thomas Aquinas**   145
  Justice and Happiness

X   **St. Thomas Aquinas and Karol Wojtyla**   151
  Intention, Person, Communion,
  Transcendence, and Mercy

Selected Bibliography   170
Index   171

Preface

In this ambitious and timely study, Sister M. Bernard Curran shows the value of studies which began with Plato and Aristotle, studies which have served as a point of departure for millennia. She is convinced that the ancients, no less intelligent or observant than we, have much to tell us about an unchanging human nature. Sister Curran skillfully leads the reader from classic sources through their modern commentaries to contemporary treatises. In the high middle ages St. Thomas was to leaven ancient insight with truths derived from Christianity. While modernity abandoned much that was Greek and Christian, not even David Hume or Immanuel Kant were willing to abandon its moral canon. The twentieth century philosophers whose work is examined here draw largely on Continental modes of thought, developing many key concepts related to moral theory. Max Scheler, Gabriel Marcel, Emmanuel Levinas and Karol Wojtyla all work within the tradition, restating basic themes in contemporary language. Current discussions of "person," "intimacy," "presence," "hope," "fidelity," "passivity" and "vulnerability" at once utilize and enrich the tradition.

At a time when the West seems to be in a period of moral and cultural decline, and that in spite of its awesome material achievements, it is prudent to turn to the past for guidance. One of the first lessons to be learned is that ours is by no means a unique period. The first century Roman historian, Titus Livius (59 B.C. to A.D. 17), better known as Livy, recommended to a failing Rome: "I invite the reader's attention to the much more serious consideration of the kind of lives our ancestors lived, of who were the men and what the means, both in politics and war, by which Rome's power was first acquired and subsequently expanded. I would have him trace the processes of our moral decline, to watch first the sinking of the foundations of morality as the old teaching was allowed to lapse, then the final collapse of the whole edifice, and the dark dawning of our modern day when we can neither endure our vices nor face the remedies needed to cure them."

Though all would admit that the present is necessarily shaped by the past, attitudes toward the inherited vary, and those attitudes in turn govern behavior. Cicero, reflecting on qualifications for leadership in the commonwealth, made a knowledge of and respect for tradition a prime requisite for office. Such knowledge is required of those who would assume positions of leadership for without it they will have no framework from which to judge. For to judge is to measure, to compare, to assess. Judging requires a standard against which a measure is taken. Livy spoke for a Rome which by the first century B.C. was already most conscious of its past: "What chiefly makes the study of history wholesome and profitable is this, that in history you have a record of the infinite variety of human experience plainly set out for all to see, and in that record you can find for yourself and your country both examples and warning."

The history of philosophical thought is indispensable because moral and other cognitive claims cannot always be directly adjudicated. Outlooks, cultures, and ways of thinking about things are not given in immediate experience, but generated through custom and learning. The process of judging can be complicated. Book length discourse is sometimes required to defend a seemingly simple observation or thesis, or to refute a claim that has been made. In spite of challenges, Western science retains the conviction, inherited from the Greeks, that nature is intelligible, that the human intellect is powerful enough to ferret out the secrets of nature, that standards can be adduced and employed.

The present study is not a moral handbook which purports to offer specific advice or solutions to concrete problems, nor is it merely an enunciation and defense of basic ethical principles. It is rather an examination of significant moral theories in which are found those distinctions, precision and definitions indispensable to moral judgment. No one can master the field of ethics without examining the thought of the authors considered herein. Sister Curran calls her book a primer, but it is a primer that leads one to sources no one can afford to neglect. Meant for students, it is nevertheless a book that can be read with appreciation by anyone who has led the examined life prescribed by Socrates.

JUDE P. DOUGHERTY
The Catholic University of America

Introduction

In *Thinkers through Time* I have tried to put together between two covers eight philosophers from Plato to the present. All eight have been enormously influential in the philosophical world and in the thought of the "man in the street." I have selected specific texts to explicate, paraphrase, quote. Some of the texts are not readily accessible to the non-professional, for example those of Scheler and Levinas, yet they are exceptionally fertile for moral understanding and more than worth the effort it takes to assimilate them.

Each chapter has a theme and each theme has been given a focus by turning it into a thesis—a modest one that is hardly arguable. These simple, even obvious, theses are not always taken for granted in contemporary life, however, and yet they are the "A, B, C's" of the ethical life. (I forego erudite distinctions between "ethical" and "moral" in favor of presenting ethics, or morality, in a way that seems to me practical.) In other words, these chapters are starters for taking seriously the themes of justice, happiness, morality, intention, person, communion, transcendence, and mercy.

The brief accounts of selections from literature as subtexts for the chapters presume the necessity of concreteness and paradigmatic figures for the deeper assimilation of principles, guidelines, and values. (I use the word "subtext" to mean "special reading" but also literal "text under the text.") The characters and events in literature are human characters and events. Literature offers an experience of moral values that is immediate.

Ordinarily, the reader participates in the literary more emotionally than he does in the philosophical.

The philosophers, selected texts, and themes of the eight chapters of Part One are as follows: I. Plato (427-347 B.C.), *Republic* I, for the theme of justice; II. Aristotle (384-322 B.C.), *Nicomachean Ethics* I, for the theme of happiness; III. St. Thomas Aquinas (1225-1274), *Summa Theologica* I-II, Question 94, for the theme of morality; IV. Immanuel Kant (1724-1804), *Critique of Practical Reason*, Chapter III, Part I, for the theme of intention; V. Max Scheler (1874-1928), *Formalism in Ethics and Non-Formal Ethics of Values*, Part II, 6B, 1, for the theme of person; VI. Gabriel Marcel (1889-1973), *Philosophy of Existentialism*, "On the Ontological Mystery," for the theme of communion; VII. Emmanuel Levinas (1906-), *Collected Philosophical Papers*, "No Identity," "Humanism and An-archy," "Philosophy and God," for the theme of transcendence; Pope John Paul II (1920-), *Dives in Misericordia*, for the theme of mercy.

The authors and titles from which the literary texts are derived are as follows: I. Sophocles (496-406 B.C.), *Antigone*; II. Sophocles, *Oedipus Rex*; III. Dante (1265-1313), *Inferno*, canto v; IV. Henrik Ibsen (1828-1906), *The Wild Duck*; V. Walker Percy (1916-1990), *The Second Coming*; VI. Karol Wojtyla (1920-), *The Jeweler's Shop*; VII. Albert Camus (1913-1960), *The Plague*; VIII. Shusaku Endo (1923-), "Mothers."

The organization of each of the chapters of Part One is as follows: first, the text from the philosopher is explicated (almost paraphrased) according to a controlling idea or thesis; second, the literary subtext is presented with comment. The notes at the end of the chapters are sometimes lengthy, but their purpose is to expand the knowledge of the subject under study and also to provide additional commentary that is interpretive.

Part Two consists of two chapters which permit the reader to reflect upon the philosophical stances of Part One. Much more work needs to be done, but here is a start, a primer.

The chapters of Part Two make use of several sources. Chapter IX treats justice by limiting the discussion to Aquinas's *Summa Theologica*, II-II, Question 58, and happiness by limiting it to I-II, Question 2.

Chapter X summarizes the theme of intention through *Summa Theologica*, I-II, Question 12, and also through Questions 18-19, as these illuminate Question 12. The same theme, intention, is examined with reference to Pope John Paul II's *The Acting Person*. The theme of person is treated through Aquinas's *Summa Theologica* I, Question 29, and relevant sections of *The Acting Person*. The theme of communion again refers to The *Acting Person* and also to *Summa Theologica*, I, Question 45, and III, Questions 60, 66, 73. For the theme of transcendence the excellent study by James F. Anderson, *Introduction to the Metaphysics of St. Thomas Aquinas*, Gateway Edition, 1969, is used, as well as *The Acting Person*. The theme of mercy in *Summa Theologica*, I-II, Question 30, is fulfilled in Pope John Paul II's encyclical *On the Mercy of God*.

From Plato and from Sophocles to the present is a long way. Change occurs. Philosophy responds to scientific and other developments. Philosophers have a penchant for redefinition and redescription. Words have their etymologies and their semasiologies. We are nevertheless instructed by the past and the present, and the human being persists.

Part One

I

PLATO
JUSTICE IS USEFUL

Plato (427-347 B.C.) was Socrates' pupil and Aristotle's teacher. As a young man, he was an admirer of Socrates and later wrote the philosophical dialogues which introduce us to the character of Socrates.[1]

Plato was born into an aristocratic family in the city state of Athens at a time of great change. Athens was at war with Sparta and was experiencing internal political, moral, and social upheaval. Plato's own relatives were among those who managed to overthrow the ruling party, but when they themselves were in power were more tyrannical than their predecessors. They attempted to connect Socrates with their activities and thus became indirectly responsible for his trial and death under the government that succeeded them. Plato left political life in disgust at the abuses he had witnessed and gave himself to the philosophical life.[2]

Plato was about thirty when Socrates died. After the death of his teacher, Plato travelled to Egypt and to Sicily, returning to Athens around 385 B.C. to found a school of research and teaching, the Academy. When Plato was in his sixties, he was invited to Syracuse to tutor its young ruler, Dionysius II. Again he found himself in a highly charged political situation. Eventually, Dion, the man who had brought him to Syracuse, was assassinated.[3] Plato was again faced with the contrast between his own theories of the state and the realities of existing states.

The first Book of the *Republic* is considered by some scholars an early dialogue.[4] It is an elenctic argument. "Elenchus" and its cognate verb, *elenchein* ("to refute, to examine critically, to censure"), are used by Socrates to describe what he does.[5]

> Socratic elenchus is a search for moral truth by adversary argument in which a thesis is debated only if asserted as the answer's own belief, who is regarded as refuted if and only if the negation of his thesis is deduced from his own beliefs.[6]

Socrates is somewhat resigned at the end of *Republic I*. He had raised the question of justice after Cephalus' discourse on old age. Cephalus had declared that having a little money, and being just and pious made old age a little easier to endure.[329d-e] Socrates has shown that justice is not what Polemarchus and Thrasymachus allege it to be; he has shown some of the other things it is not. He disavows knowledge, and disavows having found out what justice is at the end of *Republic* I. He laments that he has gotten sidetracked and not found an answer to his real question.[354b] [7]

Socrates of *Republic* I, however, refutes his interlocutors, Polemarchus and Thrasymachus, and ends up with the positive truth that justice is useful. Moreover, if certain statements are taken from the exchanges between Socrates and his interlocutors, Polemarchus and Thrasymachus, an argument can be constructed that concludes that justice is useful.

Being Truthful and Paying Debts

In a literal sense, Socrates begins where Polemarchus and Thrasymachus are. He takes up their positions so that the argument may proceed. But in another and deeper sense, Socrates begins where *he* is, that is, both knowing and not knowing that justice is useful.[8]

In the discussion with Polemarchus, the term *useful* enables Socrates to take his opponent where he would prefer not to go. Socrates does this through analogical arguments having to do with the arts and with functions.

Polemarchus has argued from the authority of Simonides that justice is telling the truth and paying back what is owed.[331d]

Socrates offers exceptions to this "rule" and thus refutes Polemarchus' position. Polemarchus has another belief, one that seems to rankle Socrates more than these first two, perhaps because it is both widely held and morally perverted. Here are Polemarchus' beliefs:

Polemarchus' belief #1: Justice is telling the truth. [331d]

Polemarchus' belief #2: Justice is paying back what is owed. [331d]

Polemarchus belief #3: Justice is rendering benefits to friends and harm to enemies. [332d]

Belief #1 and belief #2 are refuted by pointing out to Polemarchus that one would not want to tell only the truth to a madman (#1), nor would one want to return a weapon to one who was sane enough when he lent it, but not so sane when he demanded it back (#2). Socrates observes that these actions— telling the truth and paying back what is owed—can be just at one time and unjust at another time.[331c]

Benefiting Friends and Harming Enemies

It is belief #3 that Socrates refutes to establish through a lengthier elenctic argument what Socrates already knows and does not know.⁹ Beginning with the analogy between the art of medicine, then the culinary art, on the one hand, and the art of justice, on the other hand, Socrates reasons that whatever renders what is appropriate to the right person must be the art of justice. Polemarchus argues that what is appropriate for friends is good, and for enemies bad.[332d] But Socrates protests that we can be wrong about who are our friends and who are our enemies, and so can end up unwittingly doing good to our enemies and the opposite to our friends.[334e]

Socrates holds on to Polemarchus' erroneous belief about what justice is in order to show that in Polemarchus' understanding, justice is useless.[333d]

The doctor is useful to the sick; the pilot is useful to navigate the ship; the just man is useful as an ally in war. Socrates draws all three statements out of Polemarchus. But then, continues Socrates, physicians must be useless when people are well, pilots useless when not at sea, and just men useless in times of peace.[332d-333a]

Socrates now leads Polemarchus to agree that the art of farming is useful for reaping the harvest, and the cobbler's art for making shoes; then Polemarchus asserts that the just man in peacetime is useful for engagements, dealings, associations. But Socrates asks if associations of chess players, for example, require just men, or rather good chess players—the same for bricklayers, stonemasons, and harpists.[333a-b]

Polemarchus asserts that it is in financial transactions that just men are useful. Socrates' rejoinder is that in the transaction of buying and selling horses the man who owns horses would be the better partner, not the just man. Polemarchus answers that the just man is the better partner when money is to be deposited and kept safe. Socrates says that the just man must be useful when money, like scythes lying around, is useless. Socrates asks: "And so in all other cases, in the use of each thing, justice is useless but in its uselessness useful?" Justice cannot be of much value, says Socrates.[333a-e][10]

Socrates notes that Polemarchus, Simonides, and Homer all think that justice is a kind of stealing, qualified only by the fact that such stealing is for the benefit of friends and the harm of enemies. Socrates makes this remark after he has taken Polemarchus' statement that the just man is good at guarding money to argue that those who are good at guarding money must be good at stealing it, in much the same way that boxers, being good at giving blows are also good at ducking them, and doctors, being good at healing are also good at communicating disease, and generals being good at leading a march are also good at stealing one.[333c-334b]

Polemarchus by now does not know what he himself means when he says something, but he holds on to his position, or so he claims, that justice benefits friends and harms enemies. The discussion leaves justice undefined.[334b][11]

That justice is useful for the soul is not found as a "statement" in the dialogue between Socrates and Polemarchus. Socrates assumes that it is useful.[12] In the emphasis on the word "useful" in the conversation between Socrates and Polemarchus, and later on the word "advantage" in the argument between Socrates and Thrasymachus, the Platonic criticism of knowledge as something to be trained into young men is manifest. Justice is something useful and advantageous, but it is not what the Sophists think it is. Their mentality is too technical for Plato, and their morality too conventional.[13]

A statement from the Socrates-Polemarchus encounter, together with statements from the arguments between Socrates and Thrasymachus, form a small chain of reasoning that shows that justice is useful.[14]

The following are Thrasymachus' beliefs:

Thrasymachus' belief #1: Justice is the advantage of the stronger.[338c]

Thrasymachus' belief #2: Justice is a disadvantage. [339d]

Thrasymachus' belief #3: Full-scale injustice, tyranny, is the greatest advantage. [343e-344c]

Thrasymachus' belief #4: Those who fear suffering wrong revile injustice.[344c]

Thrasymachus' belief #5: Justice is simplicity, goodness of heart.[348c-d]

Thrasymachus' belief #6: Government combines injustice with power.[351b-c]

Beliefs #1, #2, #3, #4, and #6 are related to Thrasymachus' sophistical power politics, and are only consistent with each other through an understanding of justice that is what Socrates would have to try to refute: Thrasymachus first states that justice is the advantage of the stronger, and then that justice is a disadvantage.[15] He is not using words univocally, and he is using "justice" and "injustice" to mean the same thing, namely, what he is arguing for—injustice, or what amounts to injustice, since it is a perversion of justice.

Belief #5 is also a part of Thrasymachus' politics, and it is from the refutation of this belief that Socrates establishes that justice is useful. Socrates shows that the subject's obedience to his superior might lead to "the advantage of the stronger" and "the disadvantage of the stronger" being equivalent.

Thrasymachus defines "the superior" as "one in authority who does not err." This definition is Thrasymachus' "precise" definition.[340d e;341a] Should authority err, it is no longer authority, no longer the stronger, and thus does not need to be obeyed.[16]

Advantage of the Stronger

Socrates takes each art to be perfect in itself, to need nothing outside itself. He reasons that it follows that each art must be for something other than itself, for the advantage of what does not have its perfection. Thus the ruler cannot rule for his own advantage. Socrates' "precise" definitions of the physician, pilot, shepherd, ruler is "one who exercises his craft for the sake of something outside himself." Socrates has refuted Thrasymachus' belief #1.[341c-342e][17]

Disadvantage of the Stronger

Thrasymachus now insists that the just man always comes out at a disadvantage in relation to the unjust; that the ideal unjust man is the one who can be unjust on a large scale, that is, the tyrant, who, if he is not caught, is admired; that it is the fear of suffering punishment that keeps men from injustice.[339d;343e-344c]

Socrates disagrees emphatically, and accuses Thrasymachus of inconsistency, complaining that while Thrasymachus began by taking the physician in the true sense of the word, he failed to be consistent when he started to talk about the shepherd. Thrasymachus sees the shepherd as tending the sheep with a view to banqueting on them or selling them. The art of the shepherd is concerned with nothing other than the care of the sheep.

All rule, public or private, in so far as it is rule, considers what is best for nothing else than that which is governed and cared for by it. Thus we have to pay rulers, either with money, honor, or punishment if they refuse to rule.[345c-347a] Socrates has refuted Thrasymachus' belief #2, belief #3, and belief #4. [18]

Tyranny, Injustice, Power

Socrates counters Thrasymachus' belief #6 (and also #3) by asking if the city that has enslaved others, the city that Thrasymachus admires, can join in a common effort, or if it will be at odds with itself, just as the individual is, when various factions within it contend with one another. The just, then, must be more capable of action. When the unjust city, or the unjust person, does accomplish something, it is because of some justice within the city or individual.[351b-352a]

Justice a Virtue

Belief #5 (and also #4) concerns virtue and vice. Socrates accuses Thrasymachus of having views that imply justice is a vice. Thrasymachus backs down—justice is "a most noble simplicity or goodness of heart," and injustice is "goodness of judgment." The just want to outdo others but are unable to do so.

Socrates wants to examine whether or not the just have a better life and a happier one than the unjust. He asks what the function or specific work of a horse is, the function of the eye, the function of the ear, the function of the pruning-knife. The function or work of anything is that which it only or better than anything else can perform.[352c-353b]

The soul has a work, too. Its work is rule, deliberation, and life itself. The excellence of the soul is justice and its defect injustice. The just soul and the just man will live well and the unjust ill. He who lives well is blessed and happy, and he who does not is the contrary.[353b-354a] Socrates declares: "Never, then, most worshipful Thrasymachus, can injustice be more profitable than justice." [354a][19]

In his refutation of Thrasymachus' belief #5, Socrates provides the statements, which, when put together with a statement from Socrates' exchange with Polemarchus, provide the chain of thought that includes the thesis that justice is useful.
1) Justice is the specific function of man.[335d]
2) All specific functions of things are their virtues.[353b]
3) Justice is a virtue.[353c]

4) The specific function or work of man is what makes him useful.[cf.353b]
5) *What makes man* (as man) *useful is justice.*
6) The specific function of man is justice.[cf.335d]

Both implicitly and explicitly justice is shown to be useful in *Republic* I.[20]

Sophocles' *Antigone* is a play dealing with justice.[21] Antigone is one of the two daughters of Oedipus and Jocasta. Creon, the brother of Jocasta, and now king, has forbidden burial to Polynices, one of the two sons of Oedipus and Jocasta, and provided a state burial for Eteocles. Polynices and his army had attacked Thebes and Eteocles defended it. Antigone considers it impious to leave her brother unburied and intends to disobey Creon's edict. Her sister, Ismene, refuses to aid her in her design, fearing Creon and believing that she must obey the law.(A,185-90)

Creon's country is his life, as he says, and to put one's friend before one's country is to be damned, since only when the country is safe can anyone have any friends at all. Not only is Polynices not to have a grave, but he is to have no burial and no mourning. All is forbidden, and he is to be left to the dogs and the vultures. Creon says that he will never let evil triumph over good.(A,192-93)

Antigone "buries" the corpse of her brother Polynices. She puts a layer of earth over him to cover him. When Creon is told that the body has been covered over, he thinks that someone has done it for money.(A,194-98) On his orders the soldiers remove the dirt, and when Antigone finds Polynices naked again, she screams and curses and picks up some dry earth, pouring out oil from a bronze urn, and making her offering three times to the dead. The soldiers are watching, they apprehend her, and she is brought before Creon.(A,200-202)

When accused of disobeying the king's order, Antigone says that Creon's law "...was not God's proclamation."(A,203) Antigone says that God's laws are unwritten, unalterable, and everlasting. She is ready to die, willing to die, since she will do so sooner or later anyway. As it is, death will not be painful to her. If she had let her mother's son lie exposed, then she could not have borne death.(A,203)

Antigone maintains that she has a duty to the dead. Creon responds by accusing her of treating both of her brothers the same, although one was a benefactor of Thebes, and the other was a malefactor. He says that she gives honor to good and bad alike, that an enemy cannot be a friend.(A,204-206)

Antigone's response is that her way is to show her love, not her hate.(A,206)

Creon's son Haemon and Antigone are lovers. Haemon takes Antigone's side, even telling his father that Thebes is on the side of Antigone.(A,211-13)

Creon orders Antigone to be taken to a desert place, walled up inside a cave, alive, with food. This last is so that he can acquit himself of the blood guilt that would lie upon the city.(A,218)

The blind prophet Teiresias pleads with Creon to let his pride go, to pay the dead their due. Creon accuses Teiresias of wanting to get control over him for Teiresias' own material gain, which Creon says is the way of all priests. But Teiresias tells Creon that he, like all kings, seeks gain unrighteously.(A,224-27)

Teiresias prophesies that in a day or two Creon's son Haemon will die in retribution for the death of Antigone and the unburied body of Polynices. Teiresias says that nothing can undo this fate; it follows by necessity from what Creon has done.(A,227-28)

Creon goes to free Antigone and grant burial for Polynices. But he is too late. Haimon has found Antigone in a corner of the cave where she has been imprisoned. She is hanging by the neck from a rope made from her linen dress. Haimon has his arms around her. When he sees his father, he draws his sword and strikes at him. Creon flees and Haimon leans on his sword and thrusts it into his own side, again taking hold of the dead Antigone.(A,229-34)

Eurydice, Creon's wife, stabs herself before the altar, cursing her husband, Creon.(A,236-37)

At the end of the play, the Choragos intones:
> There is no happiness where there is no wisdom;
> No wisdom but in submission to the gods.
> Big words are always punished.
> And proud men in old age learn to be wise.(A,238)

Polemarchus had said that "justice is giving each his due." Creon thinks that he has given Eteocles his due, Polynices his due, and Antigone her due. Creon is "in charge," and he doles out justice according to the merits of the recipient, that is, in accord with their desert as they have done his will or not; his will is the criterion of justice. Creon believes that this form of meritocracy will ensure the strength of his government. Plato's view that doing harm to one's enemies makes them worse does not enter into Creon's account because he is not thinking of internal goods but of external goods, specifically, sheer external order. Yet Antigone, Haimon, and Eurydice do set themselves against Creon; they prefer death to life with him.

Thrasymachus holds that justice is "the advantage of the stronger." By "the stronger" Thrasymachus means someone like Creon, someone who has the power. Justice is in place if and only if what is done is in the interest of the ruling majority. In such a view, justice is actually *defined* by those in authority.

Plato thinks that rulers should work for the advantage of those ruled. Like other crafts, statecraft has as its work something or someone outside itself, in this case, the people of the city-state.

Creon thinks he is acting as a good ruler. He is in a predicament. Nothing is simple. He is caught up in circumstances that somehow overcome his intentions and acts. Nevertheless, he can be faulted for *hubris* and impiety.

To justify her actions, Antigone appeals to piety and to the gods. Her motives are familial and religious. She believes that her brother must be buried in order to enjoy eternal peace. Her political vulnerability places her in the role of heroine, but also her awe of what is beyond herself, beyond Creon, beyond Haimon and Eurydice, beyond even her brothers.

Antigone is a tragic figure, but justice is in her soul, and it is justice, not injustice, that is profitable. Justice is useful—for the soul.

Notes

1. Collinson, *Fifty Major Philosophers*, 18-19
2. Ibid., 19.
3. Ibid.
4. Plato, *The Collected Dialogues*, 575-844. The selection of Book I to answer the question of justice is partly based on its emphasis on justice in the individual soul. In Book I, Socrates has already introduced the relationship between the justice of the state and that of the individual.[*Republic* I, 347d and 351c] See Diskin Clay, in *Platonic Writings, Platonic Readings*, 24. Clay says that in Book II Plato presents ". . . Socrates' decision to project the individual soul onto the large screen of state, where its justice and injustice can presumably be seen 'writ large'." (Ibid.) As Clay shows, in the real world the individual soul is where justice can be found. "In Kallipolis, Socrates would be king, perhaps; but in Athens he is at least the ruler of the polity within the soul." (Ibid., 33)

All further references to *Republic* I will be cited in the text by line numbers and letters.

5. Gregory Vlastos, "The Socratic Elenchus," *Oxford Studies in Ancient Philosophy*, Vol. I, 1983, 27-28.

6. Ibid., 30. Vlastos is concerned that evidence for belief may fall short. In a discussion of Socrates' own claim not to know Vlastos writes:

> I have laid down sufficient conditions for fallible knowledge: where 'knowledge' = 'justified true belief', 'fallible knowledge' = 'fallibly justified true belief', i.e. true belief whose justification falls short of certainty because it rests on evidence which constitutes reasonable grounds for the belief but does not guarantee its truth. In saying that such knowledge is fallible one is not saying that one may be mistaken in believing what one knows to be true (which would be nonsense: 'I know P' entails 'P is true', as Socrates recognized [G. 454D]), but only that one may be mistaken in claiming to know this, i.e. in claiming that one has reasonable evidence for that belief and that the belief is true. See Vlastos, "Socrates Disavowal of

Knowledge," *The Philosophical Quarterly*, Vol. 35, January, 1985, Footnote 32, 13.

7. Vlastos seeks not only a conclusion of a valid argument but also premises, even starting points, that will count as knowledge, holding, understandably, that if the beginning is not true, what can be said for the ending? Since some of the disagreement concerning what kind of truth the elenchus yields has to do with disagreement about starting points or premises, some philosophers have given their attention to this problem.

Richard Kraut says that starting points as necessary to the career of an argument do not require proof. He disagrees with Vlastos when Vlastos says that the early dialogues contain only elenchic arguments that are question-begging. Kraut considers many premises in the early dialogues compelling, holding that Socrates indeed puts them under scrutiny, but that often they survive the test. Socrates just begins with empirical assumptions; he does not end with them. See Kraut, "Comments on Gregory Vlastos, 'The Socratic Elenchus,'" *Oxford Studies in Ancient Philosophy*, Vol. I, 1983, 162-65.

Vlastos's response to Kraut is to appeal to the *Gorgias* as the only dialogue in which Socrates claims that his interlocutors knew all along what the truth was, but that it took the elenchus to bring it out of them. Plato, by now more epistemological, realizes that he has to give Socrates and his interlocutors a standard—truth as consistency. See Vlastos, "Afterthoughts on the Socratic Elenchus," *Oxford Studies in Ancient Philosophy*, Vol. I, 1983, 72-74.

8. Ronald M. Polansky maintains that Vlastos has an impoverished idea of *endoxa* [opinion]. Polansky says that "endoxic propositions in the moral field...are authoritative because they are the views of the wise, and not just of anyone." See Polansky, "Professor Vlastos's Analysis of Socratic Elenchus," in *The Philosophy of Socrates: A Collection of Critical Essays*, ed. Gregory Vlastos, 252. Polansky calls for an analysis of the elenchus different from that of Vlastos. (Ibid., 259)

9. Hans-Georg Gadamer holds that the elenctic dialogues, like all the others, depend on the Socratic insight into the nature of knowing anything: remembering it. See Gadamer, *The Idea of the Good in Platonic-Aristotelian Philosophy*, 58. Gadamer's reading is a phenomenological description based on the text. (Ibid., 5)

10. Plato, through Socrates, is trying to find out what justice is, that is, what it always and everywhere is. He wants to know what "absolute" justice is. Richard Robinson says that Plato held out for "the possibil-

ity of absolute, incorrigible knowledge." But Robinson says that in the *Phaedo* Plato's hypothetical method precludes the possibility of absolute knowledge. The ruling hypothesis may always turn out to be false. Thus Plato's theory of knowledge as stated in the *Republic* is at variance with his method of attaining knowledge as outlined in the *Phaedo*. Robinson says in the *Republic* the method of attaining knowledge is by the successive destruction of each hypothesis until the unhypothesized is reached. This unhypothesized beginning is reached without images, the inquiry moving by ideas to ideas. See Robinson, "Hypothesis in the *Republic*," in *Plato I: Metaphysics and Epistemology*, ed. Gregory Vlastos, 97-101.

11. That justice is useful for the soul is not found as a "statement" in the dialogue between Socrates and Polemarchus. Nakhnikian says that only when we come to the Platonic books of the *Republic* do we see clear distinction between justice as a condition of soul and just actions, these latter being defined in terms of the former. See George Nakhnikian, "Elenctic Definitions," in *The Philosophy of Socrates: Collection of Critical Essays*, 134.

12. Leonardo Taran writes:

> The discussion with Polemarchus proceeds on two assumptions: that justice is useful and that it is good, and these assumptions Thrasymachus adopts at first. See Taran, in *Platonic Investigations*, ed. Dominic J. O'Meara, 104.

13. Gadamer, 47-48.

14. Thrasymachus was a Sophist, one of the teachers or "experts" in fifth century Greece who were reputed for their skills in rhetoric and in debate, and were sometimes deficient in sound argument. Thrasymachus as a Sophist is more politician than philosopher. Guthrie says that it is an error to neglect "the dramatic situation and emotional tension between the speakers, and the fact that the driving force behind Thrasymachus is passionate feeling rather than philosophical inquiry." See Guthrie, *The Sophists*, 91.

Kirk and Raven exclude the Sophists from their study of pre-Socratic philosophy with the following dismissal: "We have also excluded the Sophists, whose positive philosophical contribution, often exaggerated, lay mainly in the fields of epistemology and semantics." See Kirk and Raven, *The Presocratic Philosophers*, vii.

The Sophists were "wandering teachers who came to Athens from foreign cities, and sought to popularize knowledge. They came to assist young men in achieving political success." See Runes, ed., *Dictionary of Philosophy*, s.v. "Sophists."

15. Clitophon interrupts the argument. Earlier Glaucon interrupted the argument and will intervene later in Book I. Clitophon, son of Aristonymus, does not appear again after Book I of the *Republic*. Glaucon, son of Ariston, appears in other books of the *Republic* and in other dialogues. In Book II, Glaucon is a spokesman for "the ordinary run of mankind." Self-interest is what our natures pursue as a good, and it is by law or convention that we are restrained from pure self-seeking. It is human nature to wrong and to dominate others. Natural necessity requires self-indulgence of all kinds. The proponents of this view either accept these "facts of life" and call it being "realistic," or else they hold that not to follow "nature's law" is harmful. (Guthrie, 99-101)

16. The theme of justice runs through the entire *Republic*. In Book II, Socrates argues with Glaucon and Adeimantus. Here Plato presents his three classes of "beneficial things": (1) those chosen for their own sake (2) those chosen both for themselves and for their results (3) those chosen not for themselves but only for their results. The first class includes harmless pleasures; the second class, thought, sight, and health; the third, gymnastic training and being treated when ill. Glaucon says most people put being just in the third category. Thrasymachus does this in Book I. But Socrates puts justice in the second class. See Arthur Adkins in *Ethics in the History of Western Philosophy*, 14-15.

17. In the dramatic structure of the *Republic* there are four episodes. Three of the four take their form from the *agon*, the dramatic conflict between two opponents. The first episode, occupying Book I, portrays the encounter between Socrates and three others in succession: Cephalus, Polemarchus, and Thrasymachus. Socrates and Thrasymachus debate over the conception of *techne*, according to Alasdair MacIntyre. MacIntyre writes:

> For Thrasymachus . . . a *techne* is a skill or set of skills equally available to serve the interests of anyone intelligent and experienced enough to employ it. For the Platonic Socrates . . .a *techne* is a skill or set of skills directed in its exercise to the service of a good, of which the agent has to have genuine knowledge and understanding. (MacIntyre, *Whose Justice? Which Rationality?*, 72-73)

MacIntyre points out that Socrates uses the dialectic of the *elenchos* against Thrasymachus. This method, he says, is one of syllogistic argument. In such argument the conclusion follows from the conjunction of a major and a minor premise. But it is just such an absence of premises that can be agreed upon that keeps Socrates and

Thrasymachus from finding an answer to the question of what justice is. Moreover, the *elenchos* is incapable of supplying "a rationally grounded conception of goods and of the good which can claim the status of knowledge." Without some points of agreement between opponents, and without a rational method of deciding what "the good" is, one that has the status of knowledge, there is no chance of discovering what justice is, says Plato. (Ibid., 73)

18. The phrases "the entire conduct of life" and "that which would make living most worthwhile" occur in this part of the dialogue. These evoke concepts of "meaning," which for religious persons are derived from belief and moral commands. Edith Hamilton says that Greek religion was developed by poets, artists, and philosophers, rather than by priests, prophets, or saints. Poets, artists, and philosophers are people who instinctively leave thought and imagination free, and, in Greece, these types were also men of practical affairs. Greek religion was without an authoritative Sacred Book, without a creed or ten commandments, without dogma. The Greeks did not try to define the eternal and infinite, only to express it or suggest it. This they did through sculpture, poetry, and philosophy. When St. Paul said the invisible is understood by the visible, he was speaking like a Greek. Lacking a dominating church or creed, the Greeks had a dominating ideal, which different men saw differently. For the artist it was one thing and for the warrior another. "Excellence" ("virtue") is our word that is closest to this ideal, but it means the best that a man can attain to. The Greeks believed that when this excellence was perceived or caught sight of, it always had a compelling authority. See Edith Hamilton, *The Greek Way*, 208-209.

19. Here is seen the Platonic view that virtue and happiness are related. But it is important to understand Plato's conception of happiness. See MacIntyre, *After Virtue*, 131-32. MacIntyre refers to Plato's *Gorgias*, in which Gorgias and his pupil Polus are defeated in argument because of the inconsistency that results when the definition of virtue is made relative to a particular time, place, or situation. If "good," "just," and "virtue" are defined so that they refer to what brings individual success, then "justice," if it is to the advantage of the stronger, ends up meaning the same thing as "injustice," if it is to the advantage or interest of the stronger.

Callicles, in the same dialogue, is not as roundly defeated because he systematically abides by the position that domination and the satisfaction of desire without limit is "virtue." Later, Stoic philosophers, and, still later, Immanuel Kant will attempt to answer Callicles' position by separating what is good (morally) from human desires, reasoning that if what we ought to do is what satisfies our desires, and if our desires lead, as they often do, to consequences far from ordinary morality, then it must be because virtue is something quite apart from the satisfaction of desire, from success, from happiness. For Plato what is satisfying is philosophy, the love of wisdom. The concept of virtue applies to the individual, but it is primarily a political concept. Excellence as a man is excellence as a citizen, reason being the rule. (Ibid., 132) What is reason?

> That each part of the soul shall perform its specific function. The exercise of each specific function is a particular virtue. So the bodily appetites are to accept the restraint imposed by reason; the virtue thus exhibited is *sôphrosunê* That high-spirited virtue which responds to the challenge of danger, when it responds as reason bids it, exhibits itself as courage, *andreia.* Reason itself, when it has been disciplined by mathematical and dialectical enquiry, so that it is able to discern what justice itself is, what beauty itself is, and above all the other forms what the Form of the Good is, exhibits its own specific virtue of *sophia*, wisdom. These three virtues can only be exhibited when a fourth, the virtue of *dikaiosunê* is also exhibited; for *dikaiosunê*—which, on Plato's account, is very different from any of our modern conceptions of justice, although 'justice' is the translation used by almost all of Plato's translators—is precisely the virtue of allocating each part of the soul its particular function and no other.(Ibid.)

20. To say that justice has not been defined in this exchange, and yet to claim that Socrates does show that justice is useful, is at variance with positions that divide and analyze the Platonic corpus so that development of thought is emphasized to the extent that the historical Socrates is pictured as if not philosophically grown up until the *Gorgias.* Gadamer writes:

> Now that our confidence that we can discern developmental phases in Aristotle has pretty well vanished, the question forces itself upon us whether the same thing does not hold for Plato. Is there sufficient foundation for the prevailing historical-genetic view of viewing Plato's writings? (Gadamer, 8)

From the changes found in the Platonic corpus, Gadamer does not conclude, for example, that Plato came to his doctrine of ideas only later on. (Ibid., 21) He says:

> It is time that we abandoned such a naive chronological or-

dering of Plato's dialogical fiction, which in the end was tantamount to a veritable game of running back and forth from one home base to another. Instead we shall see structural similarities among groups of dialogues, so that along the way we may clarify both Plato's intentions as an author as well as the implicit content of the dialogues. (Ibid., 21-22)

21. Sophocles, *The Oedipus Cycle*, 183-244. Further references to the play are cited in the text as A.

The first section of this chapter was submitted as a paper in Dr. Timothy Roche's Seminar in Classical Philosophy in the fall of 1991 at Memphis State University. I am indebted to Dr. Roche for suggestions and subsequent changes. He is not responsible for limitations that remain, however.

Bibliography

Suggested Readings

Cavalier, Robert J., James Gouinlock and James P. Sterba, eds. *Ethics in the History of Western Philosophy*. New York: St. Martin's Press, 1989.

Hamilton, Edith. *The Greek Way*. New York: W. W. Norton & Company, 1958.

MacIntyre, Alisdair. *A Short History of Ethics*. New York: Macmillan Publishing Co., Inc., 1966.

Owens, Joseph. *A History of Ancient Western Philosophy*. Englewood Cliffs, New Jersey: Prentice-Hall, Inc., 1959.

Plato, *Republic*. Trans. Paul Shorey. In *The Collected Dialogues*, Bollingen Series LXXI. Princeton, New Jersey: University Press, 1961, 575-844.

Sophocles, *The Oedipus Cycle*. Trans. Dudley Fitts and Robert Fitzgerald. New York: Harcourt, Brace, Jovanovich, 1977.

Works by Plato

Plato's writings fall into three chronological periods according to the style in which they are written. Diogenes Laertius (III,37) says that Plato left the *Laws* unpublished. They were written on wax and copied out by a disciple, Philip of Opus. The work is thus placed in the last years of Plato's life. Starting with this dialogue, the other dialogues are arranged in chronological order according to their similarity or dissimilarity of style with this dialogue.*

The dialogues of the earliest period are the *Lysis, Laches, Euthyphro, Charmides, Hippias Major* and *Hippias Minor, Ion, Protagoras, Euthydemus, Gorgias,* and *Meno.* If Plato wrote the *Alcibiades* I and II, they are in this group. So is most of the first book of the *Republic,* perhaps originally an independent dialogue, which would have been called *Thrasymachus.*

The dialogues of the middle period are the *Timaeus, Symposium, Phaedo, Republic,* and *Philebus,* as well as the *Critias* and *Phaedrus.*

The dialogues of the third period are the *Theaetetus, Sophist, Politicus, Parmenides,* and perhaps *Cratylus.***

*Joseph Owens, *A History of Ancient Western Philosophy* (Englewood Cliffs, New Jersey: Prentice-Hall, Inc., 1959), 193-94.

**Encyclopedia of Philosophy*, Reprint Edition, s.v. "Plato."

II

ARISTOTLE
HAPPINESS IS VIRTUOUS

Aristotle was born in Stagira in 384 B.C. He went to Athens in about 367 and entered Plato's Academy as a student. He was a lecturer in the Academy, too, and left near the time of Plato's death in 347. He taught in the court of Hermias of Assos, did biological research on Lesbos with Theophrastus, and became one of the tutors of Alexander at the court of Philip of Macedonia. He returned to Athens in 335-4 to found his own school, the Lyceum or Peripatos. He left Athens in 323 because of anti-Macedonian agitation. Aristotle died in Chalcis in 332.[1]

Aristotle writes in the *Poetics:* "Tragedy is essentially an imitation not of persons but of actions and life, of happiness and misery. All human happiness or misery takes the form of action; the end for which we live is a certain type of activity, not a quality. Character gives us qualities, but it is in our actions—what we do—that we are happy or the reverse."[2]

Happiness as the Good

This view of human happiness is drawn out in the *Nicomachean Ethics*, Book I.[3] Aristotle is describing what makes for happiness, for the good life, for human flourishing. Happiness and misery take the form of action, he says in the *Poetics*. In the *Ethics* he says that all our actions aim at some good, ". . .and for this reason the good has rightly been declared to be that at which all things aim."[1094a2-3]

Thus the good does not appear to be a mood or feeling. The

pleasant mood or feeling may be an accompaniment of the action that aims at the good. Moreover, it seems that to shift the focus from the action to reflection on the action is a mistake in terms of advancing the flourishing of human beings. Such is not the case because reflection is bad; on the contrary, it is necessary. But it is no substitute for action.

Finding out what this good is at which all things aim is the concern of politics.[1094a26b5-10] By politics he means the art of living in a social group. Ordinary people and also those of "superior refinement" say that this good at which all things aim is happiness.[1095a16-20]

After disqualifying what some people think constitutes happiness—pleasure, wealth, or honor—Aristotle notes that in order to listen with profit to matters relating to politics, one must have been brought up in good habits. Those who are well brought up can get the "starting points." [lO95a20-26; lO95b15-33; 1096a1-10; 1095a30-34; 1095b1-13]

Aristotle believes that the only people who will agree with him that we seek the good in all we do are those who from early years have indeed sought the good in all they do, not because they were born doing that, but because parents and others have trained them to it. Similarly, when he asks what the good is, he relies on what the well-brought up say the good is.

Aristotle makes reference to Plato's Forms and to the Idea of the Good, only to reject these since he is unable to see how a craftsman, for example, can be a better craftsman for knowing what the Idea of the Good is. For Aristotle, the good is different in different actions and in different arts. [1096al1-35; 1096bl-36; 1097a1-14]

The good of medicine is different from the good of military strategy, the former being good as it brings health and the latter being good as it brings victory. Still, the good of medicine and the good of military strategy are alike; the good of medicine is that for which medical art is practiced, namely, health, and the good of military strategy is that for which military strategy is done, namely, victory.[1097a15-24]

Not all goods are final. Some are for the sake of something else. The chief good is something final, however. Any good less than this good is for some end beyond itself, even the good of health, which can be said to be for life's continuance. There is only one good which is desirable in itself and never for the sake of something else; that is happiness.[1097a24-36][4]

Rationality as the Function of Man

Aristotle admits that to say that happiness is the chief good is a platitude. To further clarify what this happiness is, Aristotle will try to ascertain what the function of man is.[1097b23-25]

If flute-players, sculptors, artists, carpenters, tanners have a function, man must have a function. The parts of man—eye, hand, foot—have a function. Man's function is not the life of nutrition and growth; plants have this. It is not the life of perception; horses, oxen, and all other animals have this.[1097b26-34; 1098a1-2] It is the life of reason. "There remains, then, an active life of the element that has a rational principle; . . . ."[1098a3-4]

Two meanings attach to the phrase "the rational element": man is obedient to the rational element, and man possesses the rational element and can use it. The "life of the rational element" also has two meanings: life in the sense of activity, and life in the sense of the possession of activity. It is the former, life in the sense of activity, that is closer to being the function of man.[5]

Virtue as Human Good

Aristotle reasons as follows:
> Now if the function of man is an activity of soul which follows or implies a rational principle, and if we say "a so-and-so" and "a good so-and-so" have a function which is the same in kind, e.g. a lyre-player and a good lyre-player, and so without qualification in all cases, eminence in respect of goodness being added to the name of the function (for the function of the lyre-player is to play the lyre, and that of a good lyre-player is to do so well): if this is the case, (and we state the function of man to be

27

a certain kind of life, and this to be an activity or actions of the soul implying a rational principle, and the function of the good man to be the good and noble performance of these, and if any action is well performed when it is performed in accordance with the appropriate excellence: if this is the case,) human good turns out to be activity of soul in accordance with virtue, and if there are more than one virtue, in accordance with the best and most complete.[1098a6-18]

But we must add "in a complete life." For one swallow does not make a summer, nor does one day; and so too one day does not make a man blessed or happy.[1098a19]

The preceding is offered as an outline of the good.[1098a20] He had begun with the question of the good, looked for a self-sufficing good, concluded that it was happiness, discounting pleasure, wealth, and honor, and now defines the human good as "activity of soul in accordance with virtue, and if there are more than one virtue, in accordance with the best and most complete."[6]

Aristotle will also take into account what is commonly said about the good. He has his own premises and conclusions but wants to ensure that they are in accord with the facts of experience.[1098b9-12]

Several views are run through, since "...with a true view all the data harmonize, but with a false one the facts soon clash."[1098b11-12] He appeals to the traditional views of philosophers regarding goods. Goods are divided into three classes: external goods, goods of the soul, goods of the body. The goods that relate to the soul are most properly called goods. Psychical actions and activities are in this class. Aristotle concludes that here, at least, his view of what the good is finds support. Moreover, when the end is identified with goods, it is with goods of the soul. The happy man lives well and does well, happiness being defined as a kind of good life and good action.[1098b12-22]

The following views of happiness are mentioned: virtue, practical wisdom, philosophic wisdom. One or all of these accompanied by pleasure and perhaps prosperity have to be given due credit because there is some truth in each. Yet the goods that relate to the soul, psychical goods, are most properly called goods, he has said, and it is psychical actions and activities that are in this class.[1098b12-26] ". . .for to virtue belongs virtuous activity."[1098b31]

It is not state of mind that defines happiness; it is the good result of the good state of mind. Men who are asleep or in some other way not active may possess a good state of mind, but it is only with the activity that the good result comes.[1098b32-33; 1099a1-4]

> And as in the Olympic Games it is not the most beautiful and the strongest that are crowned but those who compete (for it is some of these that are victorious), so those who act win, and rightly win, the noble and good things in life.[1099a4-5]

Virtue as Pleasant to the Noble

The life of noble men is in itself pleasant. Pleasure is a state of soul. Whatever we love is pleasant to us.[1099a7-8]

> . . .not only is a horse pleasant to the lover of horses, and a spectacle to the lover of sights, but also in the same way just acts are pleasant to the lover of justice and in general virtuous acts to the lover of virtue.[1099a9-11]

Virtuous acts are by nature pleasant.[1099a20] The lovers of what is noble find pleasant what is by nature pleasant.[1099a13-14] Thus the noble find virtue pleasant in itself.[1099a14-15] Aristotle concedes that ". . .for most men their pleasures are in conflict with one another. . .", but such is the case ". . .because these [their pleasures] are not by nature pleasant. . . ."[1099a11]

The noble person has no need of pleasure as a thing added onto life, no need of a kind of "adventitious charm" thrown in.[1099a15-16] Those who do not enjoy acting nobly are not even good. Just men enjoy acting justly. Liberal men enjoy acting liberally. Thus virtuous actions must in themselves be pleasant.[1099a17-21][7]

Happiness and Prosperity

"Happiness then is the best, noblest, and most pleasant thing in the world, ..."[1099a24-25] Yet it seems to need prosperity, the "proper equipment." Friends, riches, political power are often instruments. Good birth, good children, beauty seem necessary. For these reasons some identify happiness with good fortune.[1099b1-9]

But if happiness is just good fortune, where does that leave man with his rational principle? Aristotle thinks that most men can arrive at virtue by study and care.[1099b9-20] Indeed, it would be what he calls a "defective arrangement" [1099b24] to leave happiness to chance or to some divine providence.[1099b9,21][8]

Rationality, Virtue, Durability

A careful reading of Book I reveals that Aristotle's interest in defining happiness as virtuous activity of the soul is related to two beliefs of his: that man's distinction is rationality, and that virtue is the most durable of those things that can be desired and achieved.

Animals cannot be happy, nor even can boys. They cannot perform the required activities. We speak of boys as "happy" because we see in them great promise. The training of the rational faculty in what is good and noble is not complete in them; they do not have opportunities for the kind of activity that Aristotle has in mind for the happy man.[1099b31-32; 1100 a1-3]

The enjoyment of good and noble actions can be thwarted because activity itself can be thwarted. But it is the manner of receiving the reversals of fortune that most fundamentally mark the happy man as virtuous, and the virtuous as happy. How could man, endowed with rationality, not have some control over the greatest good: happiness? The control that is accessible is virtue.[1100a31-36;1100b1-10]

No man's life is without setbacks. Moreover, some meet with so much misfortune that it is difficult to call them happy. Nevertheless, the durability of virtue is reliable when good fortune is not.

> ...the happy man ...will be happy throughout his life; for always, or by preference to everything else, he will be engaged in virtuous action and contemplation, and he will bear the chances of life most nobly and altogether decorously, if he is "truly good" and "foursquare beyond reproach."[1100b18-21]

Sophocles' *Oedipus Rex* has as its protagonist the paradigmatic tragic hero. Oedipus is the larger-than-life man who accomplishes what would be envied had events not turned on him.[9]

The tragedy opens with Oedipus sending Creon to Delphi to obtain from the oracle some instruction that will enable him to rescue the city of Thebes from a plague. Creon returns with the command from the god to expel from Thebes "An old defilement. . ./. . .a deathly thing, beyond cure;/. . . ." [OR, Prologue,7]

Creon tells Oedipus that it was the murder of King Laios, his predecessor, that has brought on the plague. Laios had been on pilgrimage, and only one person survived the attack by a band of highwaymen. Oedipus swears to avenge the death of Laios. He had won the crown and the queen, Jocaste, by solving the riddle of the Sphinx.[10] He had delivered Thebes before; he would do it again. "Then once more I must bring what is dark to light."[OR, Prologue, 9] As he speaks to the people of Thebes, he swears to banish the discovered murderer from the city, even if he shares his own hearth, since he is "corruption itself." He associates himself with the oracle and takes the side of the murdered king.[OR, 1,13]

Oedipus is advised by the Choragos, leader of the Theban elders, or Chorus, to send for the blind Teiresias, clairvoyant to the god Apollo. Teiresias resists giving any help; he knows too much. Oedipus accuses him of being ungracious and unhelpful to his native country. But Teiresias responds to Oedipus:

> When it comes to speech, your own is neither temperate

Nor opportune. I wish to be more prudent.[OR, 1,17]

Under duress, the prophet says, "You yourself are the pollu-
tion of this country."[OR, 1,18] He tells Oedipus that he himself
is the murderer whom he is seeking, that he lives in "hideous
shame" with those most dear to him, and that he cannot see the
evil.[OR,1,19] Before he leaves, Teiresias says that the murderer
of Laios is a Theban,

A blind man,

Who has his eyes now; a penniless man, who is rich
now;
And he will go tapping the strange earth with his staff
To the children with whom he lives now he will be
brother and father—the very same; to her
Who bore him, son and husband—the very same
Who came to his father's bed, wet with his father's
blood.[OR,1,23-24]

Oedipus suspects Creon of being in collusion with Teiresias
in order to take over the kingdom. Creon tries to reason with
him, telling him that he would hardly prefer the responsibility
to the influence he now holds as Jocaste's brother. "Would any
sane man prefer/Power, with all a king's anxieties,/ To that
same power and the grace of sleep?" As king, Creon says, he
would be slave to policy. "Besides, no sober mind is treason-
able./I hate anarchy. . . ."[OR,2,29-30] Thus the balanced judgment of Creon speaks.

You do wrong

When you take good men for bad, bad men for good. A
true friend thrown aside—why, life itself Is not more
precious!
In time you will know this well:
For time, and time alone, will show the just man,
Though scoundrels are discovered in a day.[OR,2,30]

Jocaste enters and prevails upon Oedipus to desist. He
does, but without magnanimity. Creon makes his judgment:
Ugly in yielding, as you were ugly in rage!

Natures like yours chiefly torment themselves.[OR,2,34]

After Creon's exit, Oedipus questions Jocaste about Laios, and the more he hears the greater his apprehension. Oedipus tells Jocaste that Creon has charged him with the murder of Laios on the word of Teiresias. Jocaste tries to reassure him; soothsayers do not know what cannot be known. An oracle told Laios that his own son would kill him, yet he was in fact killed by a band of marauders where three highways met. Laios had been so fearful of the oracle that he had his three-day-old son's ankles pierced and tied together. He was then left to die on a mountain. Jocaste insists that prophets are useless, that God will reveal his will to them.

Oedipus asks for details of the death of Laios—how many men accompanied the king, was any of the group still alive. He learns that five were there but that only one remained, and that he had requested to be sent far from the city, where shepherds go.

Oedipus reveals to Jocaste that his own father is Polybus of Corinth, his mother, Merope, a Dorian. He tells her that once a drunken man had blurted out that he was not his father's son. Distressed, even though reassured by his parents, he visited the Delphic oracle. The god did not answer his question but instead spoke of other matters: that he would marry his own mother, have children by her, and murder his own father. He quickly fled Corinth to avoid such a fate, headed toward Thebes, came upon the chariot where three roads meet, was forced off the road by the passengers, challenged his challenger, killed him, and so must be what Teiresias says he is.

He has one hope. Jocaste has said that a shepherd survived. If the shepherd can be sent for, and his story tallies with Jocaste's—that marauders killed the king—then it was someone else that Oedipus killed, not his father.

Meanwhile, a messenger from Corinth arrives to tell of the death of Polybus. Jocaste is jubilant. The oracles are wrong again. Oedipus certainly did not kill his father. But the messenger says that Oedipus had never any worry on that account, since Polybus was not his father. A shepherd had turned Oedipus over to him and he had brought him to Corinth to the childless Polybus and Merope.

When the shepherd arrives, he admits that out of pity for the child he had been ordered to leave on the mountain, he had unfastened his ankles, and given him to the messenger to save his life. Oedipus of course has suffered from the pinning of his ankles—his name, "Oedipus," means "swollen footed."

Jocaste kills herself and Oedipus blinds himself and then exiles himself. Both are caught up in the rage that follows the revelation of "who they are." A second messenger recounts their fate.

> ... Oedipus burst in moaning and would not let us
> Keep vigil to the end: it was by him
> As he stormed about the room that our eyes were caught.
> From one to another of us he went, begging a sword,
> Cursing the wife who was not his wife, the mother
> Whose womb had carried his own children and himself.
> I do not know: it was none of us aided him,
> But surely one of the gods was in control!
> For with a dreadful cry
> He hurled his weight, as though wrenched out of
>   himself,
> At the twin doors: the bolts gave, and he rushed in.
> And there he saw her hanging, her body swaying
> From the cruel cord she had noosed about her neck.
> A great sob broke from him, heartbreaking to hear,
> As he loosed the rope and lowered her to the ground.
>
> I would blot out from my mind what happened next!
> For the King ripped from her gown the golden brooches
> That were her ornament, and raised them, and plunged
>   them down
> Straight into his eyeballs, crying, "No more,
> No more shall you look on the misery about me,
> The horrors of my own doing! Too long you have known
> The faces of those whom I should never have seen,
> Too long been blind to those for whom I was searching!
> From this hour, go in darkness!" And as he spoke,

> He struck at his eyes—not once, but many times;
> And the blood spattered his beard,
> Bursting from his ruined sockets like red hail.
>
> [OR,Exodus,66-67]

Oedipus requests exile from his successor Creon, and asks him to take charge of his two daughters, Antigone and Ismene. The sons can fend for themselves, he says. Oedipus before the city gates publicly attributes his "sad fate" to Apollo, but the gouging out of his eyes to himself. He had been determined to rid the city of plague, and he has accomplished what he set out to do. "Men of Thebes: look upon Oedipus."[OR,Exodus,78]

Oedipus seeks happiness, as do all men and women. He does not achieve it if we are to take Aristotle's characterization of a happy life as the Greek characterization. Aristotle maintains that it is only when a man's life is over that we can justly assess whether or not his life was a happy one. Since at the end of the play Oedipus has lost Jocaste to suicide, has blinded himself, and is in exile, we do not think that Sophocles is presenting him as an example of the happy man of Aristotle's *Ethics*.

We can say that accident or even "fate" brings about his downfall, and certainly fate is prominent in Greek tragedy as well as something to be reckoned with in any life. Yet the play is uninteresting if a concept of fate that leaves out human action is considered the main actor in the play.

All literature is not a type of the morality play. We in fact get deeply engaged with the action and character, scene and dialogue. We can see Oedipus as a man who by his actions is made happy or otherwise.

That Oedipus was brought up outside of Thebes was not his doing, although other human agents bore that responsibility. That he in ignorance married his own mother cannot be attributed to him as if he were deliberately incestuous. Oedipus did kill a man, and in anger, but he did not know the man was his father at the time of the murder. His actions are marked by a lack of moderation, which may indeed make him interesting, but also vulnerable.

35

"Strange, that a highwayman should be so daring—," says Oedipus to Creon in the Prologue. A few speeches later he says, "Then once more I must bring what is dark to light." One has to wonder at such a lack of self-doubt in view of the fact that Oedipus must have remembered that he himself committed a murder. Could it be that his unreflecting mind is one that inhibits the deliberation that Aristotle considers a defining characteristic of the good man, the man who will enjoy the full and happy life?

Notes

1. Burkhardt and Smith, *Handbook of Metaphysics and Ontology*, I, 50-51.
2. Aristotle, *Poetics*, 6, 16-20, translated by Ingram Bywater, in *The Basic Works*.
3. *Nicomachean Ethics* I, translated by W. D. Ross, in *The Basic Works*. Further references in text by line and letter.
4. Henry B. Veatch in "Telos and Teleology" argues for what most beginning students of Aristotle take to be Aristotelian teleology. The telos or end or goal of man is not dependent on what a particular man desires as an end or goal, but rather on what he as a man *should* desire as an end or goal. Veatch holds that any other view of teleology is not Aristotelian and ends in not being about ethics or morality at all. See Veatch, "Telos and Teleology," in *Studies in Aristotle*, 279-96.
5. Terence Irwin says that decision in Aristotle does not rest on just any kind of deliberation. Aristotelian deliberation does not depend on nonrational desire. Deliberation and decision must be about desires that are rational. The desire for happiness is such a rational desire because it ". . . includes everything we have reason to choose for itself. . . ." See T. H. Irwin, "Reason and Responsibility in Aristotle," in *Essays on Aristotle's Ethics*, 128-29.
6. An important part of the teaching on virtue is that the virtues go together. Because our own experience seems to show us that some people have certain virtues, and other people have different virtues, we tend not to take seriously this position of Aristotle's, which Socrates also had. Ackrill emphasizes that this "unity of the virtues" position has to do with a theory of the perfection of virtue. A defect in one area could have repercussions in another area. Ackrill adds that the occur-

rence of the "tragic flaw" in an otherwise admirable individual gives support to the idea that to be virtuous one must have all the virtues. See J. L. Ackrill, *Aristotle the Philosopher*, 137-38.

7. Anyone concerned about present-day confusions regarding happiness and pleasure should read Neil Postman's *Amusing Ourselves to Death: Public Discourse in the Age of Show Business*, 1986. The effect such a culture as ours has on political life is outlined in chapter 9, "Reach Out and Elect Someone."

8. Training is necessary for virtue, but for full practice reflection is required. Lear writes: "The virtuous person . . . knows who he is and who he wants to be. He is able to judge the right thing to do in a given set of circumstances and to take pleasure in doing it." See Jonathan Lear, *Aristotle: the desire to understand*, 186.

9. Sophocles, *The Oedipus Cycle*, 1-78. Further references cited in text as OR followed by scene and page number.

10. The riddle: "What has four feet in the morning, two at noon, and three at night?" Oedipus said "man," who first crawls, then is upright, and finally needs a walking stick.

Bibliography

Suggested Readings

Ackrill, J. L. *Aristotle the Philosopher.* New York: Oxford University Press. Reprint Edition, 1989.

Aristotle. *Basic Works,* ed. Richard McKeon. New York: Random House, 1941.

Lear, Jonathan. *Aristotle: the desire to understand.* New York: Cambridge University Press. Reprint Edition, 1990.

O'Meara, Dominic J., ed. *Studies in Aristotle.* Studies in Philosophy and the History of Philosophy, Vol.9, gen.ed. Jude P. Dougherty. Washington, D.C.: The Catholic University of America Press, 1981.

Postman, Neil. *Amusing Ourselves to Death: Public Discourse in the Age of Show Business.* New York: Penguin Books, 1986.

Rorty, Amélie Oksenberg, ed. *Essays on Aristotle's Ethics.* Major Thinkers Series, gen. ed. Amélie Oksenberg. Los Angeles: University of California Press, 1980.

Sophocles. *The Oedipus Cycle,* trans. Dudley Fitts and Robert Fitzgerald.

New York: Harcourt Brace Jovanovich, Harvest Book, 1977.

Works by Aristotle *

Logical works (the *Organon*)
Categories
On Interpretation (De Interpretatione)
Prior and Posterior Anaytics
Topics
On Sophistical Refutations (De Sophisticis Elenchis)

Physical works
Physics on the Heavens (De Caelo)
On Coming-to-be and Passing-away (De Generatione et Corruptione)
Meteorologics

Psychological works
On the Soul (De Anima)
Parva Naturalia: short treatises including *On Memory and Reminiscence,*
On Dreams, and *On Prophesying by Dreams*

Works on natural history
On the Parts of Animals (De Partibus Animalium)
On the Movement of Animals (De Motu Animalium)
On the Progression of Animals (De Incessu Animalium)
On the Generation of Animals (De Generatione Animalium)
Minor Treatises

Philosophical works
Metaphysics
Nicomachean Ethics
Eudemian Ethics
Magna Moralia
Politics
Phetoric
Art of Poetry

Encyclopedia of Philosophy, Reprint Edition, s.v. "Aristotle."

III

AQUINAS
MORALITY IS REASONABLE

Aquinas was born in 1225 at Roccasecca, near Naples. He was an oblate at the Benedictine Monastery of Monte Cassino from 1230 to 1239, and then a student at the University of Naples from 1239 to 1244. Having decided to become a Dominican, he studied at the University of Paris under St. Albert the Great from 1245 to 1248. He stayed in Cologne with St. Albert at the newly opened *studium qenerale* of the Dominican Order until 1252, when he returned to study at the faculty of theology in the University of Paris. There he was given the *licentia docendi* in theology and taught until 1259, when he left to teach at the papal curia in Rome until 1268. He was again at the University of Paris from 1269 until 1272, when he began teaching at the University of Naples. Saint Thomas taught and wrote for some twenty years. He died on March 7, 1274, on his way to the Council of Lyons,[1] and was canonized a saint on July 18, 1323.[2]

A crucial text for discovering the ethics of Aquinas is Question 94 in the First Part of the Second Part of the *Summa Theologica:* "Of the Natural Law."[3]

The *Summa* is written in a form intermediate between a treatise and a set of disputed questions. Like the former, it is systematic exposition of a number of topics, which includes the pertinent facts and principles and, of course, conclusions. Like the latter, it is divided into questions and answers rather than into chapters; unlike it, the multiple arguments for and against a particular thesis are replaced by difficulties which face the position Aquinas will finally adopt. Aquinas establishes his view in the "On the contrary" and "I answer that," these sections being the substantive part of the exposition. He follows with the "Replies" to the difficulties levelled against his position in the "Objections."[4]

Question 94 is sub-divided into six questions, called "Articles." They are the following:

Article 1: Whether the natural law is a habit?

Article 2: Whether the natural law contains several precepts, or one only?

Article 3: Whether all acts of virtue are prescribed by the natural law?

Article 4: Whether the natural law is the same in all men?

Article 5: Whether the natural law can be changed?

Article 6: Whether the law of nature can be abolished from the heart of man?(ST I-II, 94, Art.1-6)

We can take Aquinas's answers out of their contexts and offer a simple yes or no to each of the six questions: (1) no; (2) yes(several); (3) yes; (4) yes; (5) no; (6) no. But that would undermine the central point of Question 94, namely, morality is reasonable; our intelligence can lead us to what is right and wrong, good and bad. We can know why.

A better, even if still limited, way to understand Aquinas's thought is to examine the main body of each article, where he sets out his own position and the reasons for it.

Article 2 contains the essence of Aquinas's penetration into the connection between morality and reasonableness. Presenting the moral logic of Article 2 before treating Articles 1, 3, 4, 5, and 6 allows these other five articles to follow naturally and even inevitably from the principles in Article 2. The treatment of Article 2 will focus on Aquinas's position as it appears in the body of the article, first as "On the contrary" and "I answer that," and then will follow Aquinas's brief replies to the three "Objections" that he lists initially. Only the body of Articles 1, 3, 4, 5, 6 will be examined.

Self-evident Principles

Article 2—Whether the natural law contains several precepts, or only one?—states that there are several, just as there are several first indemonstrable principles in speculative reasoning.(ST, I-II, 94, 2, On the contrary) "The precepts of the natural law in man stand in relation to practical matters, as the first principles to matters of demonstration." In both cases there are several precepts, not one. "...the precepts of the natural law are to the practical reason, what the first principles of demonstrations are to the speculative reason; because both are self-evident principles." [Aquinas refers to Question 91, Article 3.](ST, I-II, 94, 2, I answer that)[5]

Aquinas says that something can be self-evident in two ways: in itself and in relation to us. A proposition is self-evident in itself if its predicate is contained in the notion of its subject. If a person did not know the definition of the subject, the proposition would not be self-evident to that person.(ST, I-II, 94, 2, I answer that)

The example given is the proposition "Man is a rational being." This proposition is self-evident in itself; its predicate is contained in the notion of its subject. Anyone who understands the meaning of the term "man" also understands that "man" is a "rational being." The predicate, "rational being," is contained in the subject, "man." If a person did not know the meaning of the subject term, "man," the proposition would not be self-evident to such a person.(ST, I-II, 94, 2, I answer that)

Certain propositions are universally self-evident. These are the propositions whose terms are known by everybody. Examples are the following: "Every whole is greater than its part"; "Things equal to one and the same are equal to one another."(ST, I-II, 94, 2, I answer that)

Some propositions are self-evident only to the learned. The example is that to someone who understands that an angel is not a body, it is self-evident that an angel is not limited to being in one place at a time. This is not self-evident to someone who does not know the meaning of the term "angel."(ST, I-II, 94, 2, I answer that)

Thus concludes the explanation of self-evidence, of what is indemonstrable, of what does not require demonstration or proof, an understanding of which is essential since Aquinas is basing his thought that morality is reasonable on the proposition that just as there are self-evident first principles without which nothing could be known or learned in the scientific order, so there are self-evident first principles without which nothing good can be known, learned, and done, and nothing evil can be recognized and avoided.

The First Principle of Morality

Next Aquinas explains what is necessary in order to understand what is meant by first principles of speculative reason; once this is clear, he can move to the first principles of practical reason or morality.

Aquinas says that among those things that can be apprehended by all there is an order. What is apprehended, or grasped, first, is the notion of "being." No matter what we grasp, included in it is the notion of being. Thus the first indemonstrable or self-evident principle of speculative reason is that the same thing cannot be affirmed and denied at the same time. This first principle is based on the notion of being and not-being. [Here Aquinas refers to Aristotle in *Metaphysics* IV, text 9, when he says that on this first principle all other principles of speculative reason are based.](ST, I-II, 94, 2, I answer that)

Just as being, then, is the first thing that we grasp by the speculative reason, so good is the first thing that we grasp by the practical reason. Just as the speculative reason is directed to thought or knowledge, so the practical reason is directed to action. Every agent or actor acts for an end under the aspect of good.(ST, I-II, 94, 2, I answer that)[6]

The first principle of practical reason, then, is one founded on the notion of good, namely, that good is that which all things seek after. Thus the first precept of the law is that good is to be done and pursued, and evil is to be avoided. All other precepts of the natural law are based on this first precept. Whatever the practical reason naturally apprehends as good for human beings is to be done; whatever practical reason naturally apprehends as bad for human beings is to be avoided.(ST, I-II, 94, 2, I answer that)

Good has the nature of an end, of a fulfillment.[7] Evil has the nature of a contrary of a fulfillment, as a frustration of an end or a fulfillment. Thus all that human beings have a natural inclination toward, reason judges to be good, and so objects of pursuit. What reason judges to be bad are objects of avoidance. The precepts of the natural law, then, follow the order of natural inclinations.(ST, I-II, 94, 2, I answer that)

The following precepts follow from the first one:

First, in human beings is the inclination to good that human beings have in common with all other substances, natures, or essences not human: the preservation of their own being. Whatever is a means of preserving human life and of warding off obstacles to that life is from this natural law.

Second, in human beings is that good which they have in common with other animals. This good is in the form of inclination, for example, the inclination toward sexual intercourse and the care and education of offspring from such union.

Third, in human beings there is an inclination to good because of their rational nature. Thus humans have a natural inclination to know the truth about God and to live together in society. These inclinations are from the natural law in human beings by which they try to avoid offending those among whom they have to live.(ST, I-II, 94, 2, I answer that)

The natural law is one law since all the precepts flow from one first precept: good is to be done and pursued, evil is to be avoided.(ST, I-II, 94, 2, Reply Obj. 1)

All of the human inclinations, those having to do with desire of any kind, as well as those having to do with repugnance, in so far as they are ruled by reason, are part of the natural law. Morality is reasonable; human intelligence can be used correctly and human beings can be good.(ST, I-II, 94, 2, Replies Obj. 2-3) The remaining five articles of Question 94 outline a consistent insight into the nature of morality.

The Habit of Morality

The body of Article 1—Whether the natural law is a habit?—first quotes Augustine [*De Bono Conjug.* xxi] to say that ". . . a habit is that whereby something is done when necessary." Aquinas reasons that since the natural law is in both infants and the damned, and these cannot act by it, natural law cannot be a habit.(ST, I-II, 94, 1, On the contrary)

Aquinas then distinguishes between the two ways a thing may be called a habit: 1) A habit, understood in its proper and essential sense, is that by which we act, rather than an act, such as an act of reason. But the natural law is as much an act of reason as a proposition is. Thus the natural law cannot be properly called a habit. 2) A habit may be so termed to mean that which we hold by habit. In this second sense, the natural law can be considered a habit.(ST, I-II, 94, 1, I answer that)

When we say that the natural law is "in" us, we mean that it is both a work of reason in us and a habit of reason in us. As a work of reason, the precepts of the natural law are "considered" or thought about by reason. When we reflect on what is good for human beings and what is bad for them, we are doing a work of reason, and are freely considering what will tend toward human flourishing and what will hinder that flourishing. As a habit of reason, for instance, having the habit of a precept of the natural law, human beings simply do what is good for them and abstain from what is bad for them.

The Naturalness of Virtue

Article 3—Whether all acts of virtue are prescribed by the natural law?—in the "On the contrary," presents a quotation from Damascene [*De Fide Orthod.* iii.4]: ". . .virtues are natural."(ST, I-II, 94, 3, On the contrary)

In his discussion, Aquinas distinguishes between two aspects of virtuous acts. The first aspect is virtuous acts considered as virtuous, that is, as excellent and proper for a reasonable being to perform. All acts of virtue considered this way are prescribed by the natural law.(ST, I-II, 94, 3, I answer that)

The second way to consider virtuous acts is to consider them in themselves, that is, as particular kinds of virtuous acts. Since nature does not at first incline toward some of these, they are not said to be prescribed by the natural law. It is only through the inquiry of reason that they have been found to be conducive to human well-being.(ST, I-II, 94, 3, I answer that)

Is it natural to be virtuous? From one point of view it is; from another point of view it is not. It is natural to be virtuous because it is reasonable to be virtuous, but the practice of virtue is not necessarily natural for human beings. It is only through investigation that human beings know that such acts conduce to their well-being.

The Universality of the Law

In the body of Article 4—Whether the natural law is the same in all men?—Aquinas appeals to Isidore [*Etym.* v.4]: "The natural law is common to all nations."(ST, I-II, 94, 4, On the contrary)[8]

Aquinas maintains that the natural law is the same in all people, common to all nations. The natural law within us inclines us to whatever is natural to human beings. Among what is natural is the inclination to act according to reason.(ST, I-II, 94, 4, I answer that)

The process of reason is from the common to the proper, from the general to the particular. [Here Aquinas refers to Aristotle's *Physics* i.](ST, I-II, 94, 4, I answer that)

Speculative reason works differently from practical reason. Speculative reason is chiefly concerned with necessary things, things which cannot be other than they are. Its conclusions, therefore, reach the truth without fail. Practical reason is concerned with contingent matters, matters that do not have to be as they are. Human action is concerned with these matters. There is necessity in the general principles of practical reason, but the more we come to matters of detail, the more we encounter what Aquinas calls "defects."(ST, I-II, 94, 4, I answer that)

When we come to the details, truth or "practical rectitude" is not the same for all. Again, the general principles are the same for all, but not the working out of the details that follow on the general principles.[9] Moreover, even when rectitude would be the same for all with regard to the details of an action, what is right is not known equally by all.(ST, I-II, 94, 4, I answer that)[10]

The general principles of both speculative reason and practical reason are the same for all. No one can affirm and deny the same thing at the same time—no knowledge could be had did this general principle of speculative reason have an exception. Good is to be done and pursued and evil avoided by all—no morality could be secured did this general principle of practical reason have an exception.

These general principles are not only known by all, but they are the same for all.(ST, I-II, 94, 4, I answer that)[11] The conclusions of the general principles of speculative reason are the same for all but are not known to all. For example, it is true for everyone that the three angles of a triangle are together equal to two right angles, but everyone does not know this.(ST, I-II, 94, 4, I answer that)

The conclusions of practical reason are not always the same for all, and when they are the same, they are not known to all. A general principle of practical reason is that it is right to act according to reason. We can conclude from this that goods entrusted to another should be restored to their owner. This conclusion applies to the majority of cases. In some particular cases, however, to restore goods to the owner may be injurious. The example Aquinas gives of such an injurious restoration of goods is when the goods restored might be used to fight against one's own country.(ST, I-II, 94, 4, I answer that)

The more we get into details regarding the restoration of goods, the more the general principle fails; for example, if we say that the restoration should be with a certain guarantee, or take place in a certain way. The more conditions added, the more likely is it that the general principles will fail.(ST, I-II, 94, 4, I answer that)

Aquinas maintains that in most cases the conclusions are the same. He says that the few cases that fail do so because of some obstacle so that even natures subject to generation and corruption may not always be so subject. He says that in some few

46

cases people may not know what the conclusions of practical reason are. Their reason may be perverted by passion, evil habit, or by some evil disposition of nature. Aquinas tells us that Julius Caesar relates in *On the Gallic Wars*, vi, that at one time the Germans did not consider theft wrong.(ST, I-II, 94, 4, I answer that)

The Unchangeableness of the Law

Article 5—Whether the natural law can be changed?—cites in the "On the contrary" of the Article, the Decretals [*Dist.* v]: "The natural law dates from the creation of the rational creature. It does not vary according to time, but remains unchangeable."(ST, I-II, 94, 5, On the contrary)

Aquinas says that a change in natural law may be understood in two ways: by addition and by subtraction. Things can be added to the natural law, for example, by Divine law and by human laws. With regard to subtraction, it is unchangeable in its first principles.(ST, I-II, 94, 5, I answer that)

Aquinas makes a distinction regarding secondary principles. He maintains that the detailed proximate conclusions drawn from the first principles cannot be changed in such a way that what it prescribes is not right in most cases. With regard to some particular cases of rare occurrence, it can be changed. But he makes it clear that he is referring to the hindrance to the observance of such secondary precepts by special causes. Here he refers to Article 4, which shows that as conditions are added, the conclusions will not follow as successfully from the general principle. Ignorance, passion, habit, or disposition of nature can lead to such non-observance of such secondary precepts.(ST, I-II, 94, 5, I answer that)

The Law in the Heart

Article 6—Whether the law of nature can be abolished from the heart of man?—in the "On the contrary" of the question, relies on the authority of Augustine [*Conf.* ii] "Thy law is written in the hearts of men, which iniquity itself effaces not."(ST, I-II, 94, 6, On the contrary)

The general principles of the natural law, considered abstractly, can never be blotted out from men's hearts, Aquinas says. The general principles can be blotted out in the concrete, in a particular action, when reason is hindered from applying the general principle to a particular practice because of concupiscence or some other passion. [Here Aquinas refers to Question 77, Article 2, where he maintains that reason can be overcome by passion and against its own knowledge.](ST, I-II, 94, 6, I answer that)

Moreover, the secondary precepts of the natural law can be blotted out from the human heart by evil persuasions, just as in speculative matters errors occur with regard to necessary conclusions. The natural law can be blotted out from the human heart with regard to the secondary precepts by vicious customs and corrupt habits. Aquinas notes that among some men theft and even unnatural vices are judged not to be sinful, and he refers to the First Letter of Saint Paul to the Romans.(ST, I-II, 94, 6, I answer that)

Aquinas's position on natural law is found in the context of his understanding of law in general, the essence of which is reason. Morality has to do with law; law has to do with reason; morality is reasonable; reason is from God.

The Divine Comedy by Dante Alighieri is a medieval masterpiece extolling reason and virtue. In literature it is the parallel to the theology of Aquinas.

The soul of the poet-pilgrim, Dante, is guided by the poet Virgil, and others, through the regions of hell, purgatory, and, finally, to heaven. In the *Inferno,* canto v, "The Carnal," the poet Dante tells us the story of Paolo and Francesca.[12] Canto v opens the section called the Second Circle, the beginning of Hell proper, cantos i-iv having treated "The Dark Wood of Error," "The Descent," "The Vestibule of Hell," and "Limbo"—Circle One.

In canto v of Dante's *Inferno,* the souls are whirled and battered. They shriek their way around hell blaspheming the power of God.[13]

Dante asks Virgil:

> . . .Teacher, tell me, what souls are these
> punished in the sweep of the black wind?[14]

Francesca and Paolo are spinning within a great whirlwind with the other souls of the carnal, those who betrayed reason to their appetites. Their sin was to abandon themselves to the tempest of their passions. Not only was their union not legitimated by marriage, but Francesca was the wife of Gianciotto, Paolo's older brother. Thus they are swept eternally in the tempest of Hell, denied the light of reason and of God.[15]

Dante, the pilgrim through the infernal regions, accompanied by his guide, the poet Virgil, asks Paolo and Francesca in the name of love to tell their story. Francesca tells it while Paolo weeps at her side. Dante is overcome by emotion and swoons when he hears their tale. Dante, the pilgrim, not the poet, does not know the nature of sin at this stage of the *Inferno*.[16]

Francesca speaks:

> . . .Love, that kindles quick in the gentle heart, seized
> this one for the beauty of my body, torn from me. (How
> it happened still offends me!)
>
> Love, that excuses no one loved from loving, seized me
> so strongly with delight in him that, as you see, he never
> leaves my side.[17]

Paolo and Francesca were making love when her husband (his brother) walked in on them. Gianciotto murdered them on the spot, giving them no chance to repent.

Francesca tells how they were one day reading together the story of Lancelot and Guinivere, and how love had mastered these two. Francesca and Paolo were alone.

> . . .Time and again our eyes were brought together by
> the book we read; our faces flushed and paled. To the
> moment of one line alone we yielded:

it was when we read about those longed-for lips now being kissed by such a famous lover, that this one (who shall never leave my side)

then kissed my mouth, and trembled as he did. Our Galehot was that book and he who wrote it. That day we read no further.[18]

The sins of the carnal in the Second Circle of the *Inferno* are punished with eternal damnation. The damned suffer pain, ". . .stinging the soul to wailing."[19] Minos, the semi-bestial judge who assigns to each soul its eternal torment, awaits them. He delivers his verdict with his coiling tail.

There stands Minos grotesquely, and he snarls, examining the guilty at the entrance; he judges and dispatches, tail in coils.[20]

Virgil says the first is Semiramis, the Sultan queen. Dido, faithless to Sechaeus, killed herself for her lover. Cleopatra, "who loved men's lusting" is there, as are Helen, Achilles, Paris, and Tristan, and many others—all sinners against reason in letting go of it for sexual passion.[21]

Dante as pilgrim, lacking at this stage of his journey the appropriate hatred of sin, seems somewhat sympathetic to the lost lovers. Francesca plays on our feelings by her words, and Paolo by his silence.[22]

The *Inferno* is best read in its entirety and with the *Purgatorio* and *Paradiso*. In the context of the whole narrative the faith/reason paradox reveals itself and places acts against reason in the darkness where no light of reason shines. In the *Paradiso* Dante is led to the experience of the fruit of reason, the vision of God, and the fruit of love, union with God.

The classical mind sees literature as having the functions of delighting or entertaining, but also of instructing, teaching. We can draw what conclusions we choose within the parameters set by the literary text.

Francesca and Paolo had within them the natural law, the first principle of which is that good is to be done and evil avoided. They offended in a serious matter; they are both adulterers, and Paolo could also be classified as a betrayer of a close relative. Since his motivation is concupiscence, however, his sin is carnal. By the natural law, people have the right to co-habit, but not outside of a permanent bond that ensures (1) fidelity to a person as an end in himself, not merely as a means to pleasure, and (2) the well-being of possible offspring.

One might say that what Francesca and Paolo did was "natural." It is natural to be attracted to some other person, and natural for such attraction to seek and achieve union. Such "naturalness," however, omits the reflection on one's behavior that is the dignity and the obligation of the human being. Sins of the flesh are "natural" when considered as the result of a natural procreative urge. These sins are against the natural law in so far as they result from a neglect of the use of practical intelligence, and indicate the absence of the virtue of chastity.

The Francesca and Paolo scenario would have been different had these two employed the powers of their speculative reason with its understanding of natural necessity. Such a suggestion might sound cold and unsympathetic, even ridiculous. Yet it is just such discipline that couples attracted to one another exercise when they choose *not* to read love stories (or engage in similar activities) that will inevitably arouse feelings that cannot legitimately be satisfied.

Besides the fact that all the world does love lovers, Francesca and Paolo enlist sympathy because they are young, and the husband in the case is ugly. Aquinas says that reason may be perverted by passion, habit, or evil disposition. Passion seems to have deranged reason in this case. The deformity of the husband could be considered an "evil disposition," at least as the lovers perceived it, but what Aquinas means is "evil disposition" on the part of sinners. Extreme ugliness repels, however, so that the lovers' guilt, although not sufficiently mitigated to keep them out of Dante's Hell, does evoke pity.

What twists "natural apprehension," the apprehension that their liaison is too evil and so very bad for them, is ignorance.

Ignorance of what? Ignorance of the love of God. It is indeed hard to see how these two could have had a way out without the love of God, which is grace.

Notes

1. Runes, 31.
2. Weisheipl, 349.
3. St. Thomas Aquinas, *Summa Theologica*, Ia IIae, Q.94, 1981. All further references to this part of the *Summa* will be cited in the text as ST, I-II, 94, followed by the article number and either "On the contrary" or "I answer that."

It is important to note here that Aquinas's presentation of natural law in this section of the *Summa* cannot fairly be isolated from his other moral and thus theological analyses in the *Summa* and in his entire corpus.

For the faithful interpretation of the mind of St. Thomas in moral theology, the following should be consulted: Francesco Roberti, comp., and Pietro Palazzini, ed., *Dictionary of Moral Theology*, trans. Henry J. Yannone, Westminster, Maryland, Newman Press, 1962, and Battista Mondin, *Dizionario Enciclopedico del Pensiero di San Tommaso*, Bologna, ed. Studio Domenicano, 1991.*

4. Kenny, *Aquinas*, 15.
5. For some philosophers, for example, William of Ockham (c. 1285-1349), the question of evidence, and so of self-evidence, becomes the crucial question. According to Ockham, the universal propositions of scientific demonstrations are formed only from concepts by which things are apprehended abstractively and without evidence of their existence. [Aquinas holds that truth is primarily in the intellect, thus in concepts and propositions, but that these are founded in things; our senses provide evidence of the existence of things.]

According to Ockham, self-evident propositions are necessary only if they are understood as conditionals or as propositions concerning the possible. Also, such propositions may be evident by the meaning

---

* My deep respect and gratitude go to Luigi Cardinal Ciapi, O.P., for reading this chapter and for suggesting the two sources in Note 3, paragraph 3.

of the terms in the propositions or by experience. Premises in mathematical demonstrations and premises in the natural sciences are evident by the meaning of the terms of the propositions.

Also, in the natural or physical sciences there are premises that are established by generalization from singular contingent propositions evident by intuitive cognition, for example, those that state causal laws. ["Intuitive cognition" is like the sense knowledge of Aquinas.] But Ockham considers such premises hypothetical, not absolute, since it is logically possible for the effect not to follow on the usual cause. See *Encyclopedia of Philosophy*, Reprint Edition, s.v. "William of Ockham."

Ockham, like Descartes later, and unlike Aquinas, requires that all truth be tested mathematically and/or logically. Aquinas as a "moderate realist" has a greater confidence in the evidence of the senses, even though he is aware that they can be unreliable. Perhaps more important is Aquinas's more complex understanding of different kinds of truth.

6. The critics of this view would hold that for it to be acceptable, ordinary meaning has to be bent. It is clear that some people act for an evil end; for example, in a case of premeditated murder, the end is evil. For this "evil end" to be seen as an "apparently or seemingly good end," the removal of an unwanted person, which is what the perpetrator of the crime intends, is to bend meaning.

Some, also, for strictly religious reasons do not agree with Aquinas here, their reason being that people can be influenced by the devil, other people, or the malice in their own hearts to will an evil end. Aquinas, of course, knows this, but still maintains that all seek at least what seems good to them for some reason.

7. Kant will reject the idea that moral good has the nature of an end or a fulfillment. For an action to be moral it must be done from duty. We may have a duty to try to be happy, to live a fulfilling life, but morality is not equated with happiness or human fulfillment.

8. The view that the natural law is essentially the same for all is contradicted by what is known as "cultural relativism." The definition of this offered by Oliver A. Johnson is the following: "The theory that there are no universal or absolute moral standards, but that all such standards are relative to the particular culture that accepts them and so have no validity outside that culture. A form of *ethical skepticism*." See Johnson, "Glossary," 446.

9. Aquinas of course is not teaching moral relativism or subjectivism. "Moral relativism holds that there are no unchangeable principles of

human behavior, either because all truth is relative or because there are no inherently evil actions, since everything depends on other factors, such as customs, conventions, or social approval." John A. Hardon, S.J., *Modern Catholic Dictionary*, 461.

Johnson defines "radical subjectivism" as follows: "The theory that normative ethical propositions are really pseudo-propositions, incapable of being true or false, and so are cognitively meaningless, or nonsense. A form of ethical *skepticism*." Johnson, "Glossary," 448.

10. Circumstance mitigates and thus the circumstance of ignorance, even partial, mitigates. "Circumstance. As one of the determinants of morality, something that either accompanies or is missing from a human act and thereby modifies its merit or gravity or the person's responsibility." (Hardon, 107)

11. Perhaps the most noteworthy of the recent treatments of natural law is John Finnis, *Natural Law and Natural Rights*, 1986. But also see Alasdair MacIntyre's most recent works, especially *Three Rival Versions of Moral Enquiry*, 1990, where Nietzsche has to face Leo XIII's *Aeterni Patris*. Also, because of the bearing on moral issues of modern epistemology, Yves A. Simon's *An Introduction to Metaphysics of Knowledge*, 1990, is essential.

12. Dante, *The Divine Comedy*, Vol.I: *Inferno*, trans. Mark Musa, 1984.

13. In the *Paradise* the souls in heaven also spin, but their spin is a dance. The Seraphim and Cherubim, the first two rings of angels, along with the others, dance and sing "Hosanna." [Vol.III, trans. Mark Musa, 1986, canto xxviii, 11.94-99.]

> They spin so swiftly speeding in their bonds to grow as much like that Point as they can, and they can in proportion to their sight. (11.100-102)

They see God ["...the Fixed Point that holds each to his ubi,/the place they were and will forever be."] (11.95-96) to the extent that they desire to be like Him, and their speed is in proportion to their fervor. Vision precedes love and vision belongs to the intellect and reason. Love, an act of the will, follows on vision.

> And know that all of them delight in bliss according to how deep their vision delves into the Truth in which all minds find rest.(11.106-108)

14. *Inferno*, canto v, 11.50-51.

15. In the *Purgatory* penitents of lust are placed in Upper Purgatory just before the Earthly Paradise. Their sins were excessive love of persons. Every sin is a sin of love. Thus love itself has to be purged.

"Disordered love of Good"—excessive love of secondary good, God being Primary Good, was their sin.

The souls in purgatory want to be there. The punishments are purgative, not penal. They end as soon as the interior of the soul is cleansed. These souls will eventually enjoy the vision and love of God because they have repented of their sins against love. (All sins and all virtues are rooted in love.) Cf. *Purgatory,* trans. Dorothy Sayers, 1955, Introduction, 67; Commentaries, 276.

Sayers says on p. 67: "It will be noticed that, as in Hell, the warmer-hearted sins which involve exchange and reciprocity are at the top, and the cold egotism which rejects community is at the bottom."

16. Cf.Inferno, canto v, Notes, 114.

17. *Inferno,* canto v, 11.100-105.

18. *Inferno,* canto v, 11.130-38.

19. *Inferno,* canto v, 1.3.

20. *Inferno,* canto v, 11.4-6.

21. Cf. *Inferno,* canto v, 11.52-72.

22. See the discussion of the punishment of Francesca and Paolo in Musa's Notes to *Inferno,* canto v, 114-20. Their being together is a heavy part of their punishment.

Bibliography

Suggested Readings

Aquinas, Thomas. *Summa Theologica,* Volume II. Translated by Fathers of the English Dominican Province. Westminster, Maryland: Christian Classics, 1981.

Dante Alighieri. *The Divine Comedy,* Volume I: *Inferno.* Translated by Mark Musa. New York: Penguin Classics, 1984.

——————— . *The Divine Comedy,* Volume II: *Purgatory.* Translated by Dorothy L. Sayers. New York: Penguin Classics, 1955.

——————— . *The Divine Comedy,* Volume III: *Paradise.* Translated by Mark Musa. New York: Penguin Classics, 1986.

Weisheipl, James A., O.P. *Friar Thomas D'Aquino: His Life, Thought, and Work.* Garden City, New York: Doubleday, 1974.

Major Works by Aquinas *

(a) *Scriptum in IV Libros Sententiarum* (1254-1256), *Summa Contra Gentiles* (c. 1260), *Summa Theologica* (1265-1272);

(b) commentaries on Boethius (*De Trinitate,* c. 1257-1258), on Dionysius the Pseudo-Areopagite (*De Divinis Nominibus,* c. 1261), on the anonymous and important *Liber de Causis* (1268), and especially on Aristotle's works (1261-1272), *Physics, Metaphysics, Nicomachean Ethics, Politics, On the Soul, Posterior Analytics, On Interpretation, On the Heavens, On Generation and Corruption;*

(c) *Quaestiones Disputatae,* which includes questions on such large subjects as *De Veritate* (1256-1259); *De Potentia* (1259-1263); *De Malo* (1263-1268); *De Spiritualibus Creaturis, De Anima* (1269-1270);

(d) small treatises or *Opuscula,* among which especially noteworthy are the *De Ente et Essentia* (1256); *De Aeternitate Mundo* (1270), *De Unitate Intellectus* (1270), *De Substantiis Separatis* (1272)

---

* Runes, 31.

IV

KANT
INTENTION IS DECISIVE

Immanuel Kant was born in 1724 at Konigsberg in East Prussia, the son of a saddler, and, by his own account, the grandson of an emigrant from Scotland. Kant was educated at a high school in Konigsberg, and then the Collegium Fridericianum. But it was at the University of Konigsberg that Kant met an exceptional teacher in the person of the philosopher Martin Knutzen.[1]

Kant left the university in about 1746 and was employed for a few years as a tutor in families in various parts of East Prussia. He continued his studies, however, and in 1755 took his master's degree at Konigsberg and began to teach in the university as a *Privatdozent*. He taught physics, mathematics, physical geography, and philosophy. Kant remained poor for all of this time, and it was not until he was appointed in 1770 to the chair of logic and metaphysics at Konigsberg that his financial circumstances altered.[2]

Kant first published in 1747, and continued to publish, but not until after 1760 did he begin to think in philosophy in a way that would lead to the more revolutionary philosophy for which he is admired. From 1770 on he worked on the *Critique of Pure Reason*, bringing it out in 1781. Because it was greeted with bewilderment, he followed it with several works that he hoped would elucidate his central ideas. He continued to work out the rest of his philosophical system.[3]

By around 1797 Kant was enjoying much acclaim in Germany and was beginning to be studied in other countries. In his last years, however, Kant suffered the criticisms of younger philosophers who claimed that he did not understand his own system and inaugurated "transcendental" systems of their own. There is reason to believe that he was attempting to answer these objections, but he left only fragments, collected under the title *Opus Postumum*.[4]

Kant led a quiet life, never married, lectured dutifully as a professor, met with his friends, and took care of his health—he remained in good health until shortly before his death in 1804.[5]

In Kant's *Critique of Practical Reason*[6] is a section called "Analytic of Pure Practical Reason." Chapter III, entitled "The Incentives of Pure Practical Reason," contains six specific references to "intention" that reveal with a certain directness Kant's more apparent "intention" (motive, spirit) in positing "intention" as decisive with regard to the moral worth of actions, or the "moral law." (CPrR,75-87) These references are found in the first part of Chapter III, excluding the discussion of "personality," and before the section "Critical Elucidation of the Analytic of Pure Practical Reason." (CPrR, 74-90)

These six references to "intention" can be distinguished one from the other by their contexts so that an examination of them can be made under the following topics: (1) letter and spirit; (2) the law of duty; (3) desires and inclinations; (4) moral fanaticism. Two of the six come under (2) the law of duty, and two others of the six come under (4) moral fanaticism.

Letter and Spirit

The first reference to "intention" is found in a footnote. It reads as follows:

> Of every action which conforms to the law but does not occur for the sake of the law, one may say that it is morally good in letter but not in spirit (in intention).(CPrR, 75, footnote 1)

This footnote of Kant's follows his explanation of his understanding of "incentive."

Now, if by an incentive (*elater animi*) we understand a

subjective determining ground of a will whose reason does not by its nature necessarily conform to the objective law, it follows, first, that absolutely no incentives can be attributed to the Divine will; and, second, that the [moral] incentive of the human will (and that of every created rational being) can never be anything other than the moral law; and, third, that the objective determining ground must at the same time be the exclusive and subjectively sufficient determining ground of action if the latter is to fulfill not merely the letter of the law but also its spirit.(CPrR, 74-75)

The fact that Kant uses "intention" and "spirit" as either explanations of each other or as synonyms is related to his statement that the Divine will cannot have incentives attributed to it. Since an "incentive" is "a subjective determining ground of a will whose reason does not by its nature necessarily conform to the objective law," God and incentives cannot be conjoined. It is the "created rational being" whose will can have only one moral incentive, the moral law, because this being's reason does not by its nature necessarily conform to the objective law.

Again, because the "created rational being" has a reason which does not by its nature necessarily conform to objective law, the objective determining ground of the will of the "created rational being" must also be the "exclusive and subjectively sufficient determining ground of action." It is if, and only if, the ground of action, considered subjectively, has the same incentive as the ground of action, considered objectively, that is, the moral law, that the "spirit" or "intention" of the law is fulfilled. The law alone is the "elater animi" for the confluence of letter and spirit, without which confluence nothing is moral.

The emphasis on the [natural] limitation of the "created rational being" with regard to conformity to objective law will be reiterated in the remaining five references to "intention," especially under the rubric of "moral fanaticism." God does not have incentives; He does not have the moral law as sole incentive for conformity to letter and spirit of that law; He does not need this "intention" or "spirit" because He is without the limitation of the "created rational being." God is one and perfect, without cleavage between reason and act. For the "created rational being," however, intention is decisive in the following strict sense: no act is moral unless it is done *from* the intention of conformity to the moral law.(CPrR, 84-85)

The "created rational being" has a reason that is flawed; he needs the incentive, the moral law, in order to conform to the moral law in letter and spirit. Moreover, without this incentive, without the "elater animi," no act of the "created rational being" can be moral.

The Law of Duty

In his discussion of the law of duty, two references to "intention" occur—the second and third such references in this first part of "The Incentives of Pure Practical Reason." Kant writes:

> The moral law is, in fact, for the will of a perfect being a law of holiness. For the will of any finite rational being, however, it is a law of duty, of moral constraint, and of the determination of his actions through respect for the law and reverence for its duty. No other subjective principle must be assumed as incentive, for though it might happen that the action occurs as the law prescribes, and thus in accord with duty but not from duty, the intention to do the action would not be moral, and it is the intention which is precisely in question in this legislation.(CPrR, 84-85)

The intention is not moral unless it is respect for the law, reverence for the duty of the law. If the intention is not moral, the moral law is not done. The law of duty is the only subjective principle that may be an incentive for an action to be called a moral one. Finite rational beings are beings whose wills are not perfect. Thus the moral law for them is one of duty, of moral constraint—of keeping the law from duty, from the intention of simply keeping the law. For the will of a perfect being the moral law is one of holiness.

Created, finite rational beings cannot be holy, but they can be moral—if their intention is to act solely from duty when they keep the law.

Desires and Inclinations

The fourth reference to "intention" is best understood in the context of the passage in which it appears at the end and as a conclusion to an argument.

> If a rational creature could ever reach the stage of thoroughly liking to do all moral laws, it would mean that there was no possibility of there being in him a desire which could tempt him to deviate from them, for overcoming such a desire always costs the subject some sacrifice and requires self-compulsion, i.e., an inner constraint to do that which one does not quite like to do. To such a level of moral disposition no creature can ever attain. For since he is a creature, and consequently is always dependent with respect to what he needs for complete satisfaction with his condition, he can never be wholly free from desires and inclinations which, because they rest on physical causes, do not of themselves agree with the moral law, which has an entirely different source. Consequently, it is with reference to these desires always necessary to base the intention of the creature's maxims on moral constraint and not on ready willingness, i.e., to base it on respect which demands obedience to the law even though the creature does not like to do it, and not on love, which apprehends no inward reluctance to the law by the will.(CPrR, 86-87)

Special notice should be taken of how Kant understands "love" in this passage. "Love," "like," "desire," "inclination," "the will"––are given meaning by Kant by his use of them in this discussion of the necessity of respect for the law. No one of these appears to play an active or positive part in the duty of obedience to the law. Kant sees them as relating to "satisfaction," to the "physical." For Kant the moral law has "an entirely different source."

The previous paragraph from Kant again shows that he is unwilling to maintain that creatures can love the law.

> This would be true even if the mere love for the law (which would in this case cease to be a command, and morality, subjectively passing over into holiness, would cease to be virtue) were made the constant but unattainable goal of its striving. For in the case of what we esteem and yet dread because of our consciousness of our weaknesses, the most reverential awe would be changed into inclination, and respect into love, because of the greater ease in satisfying the latter. At least this would be the perfection of a disposition dedicated to the law, if it were possible for a creature to attain it.(CPrR, 87)

Moral Fanaticism

The last two references to "intention" are in a section the main purpose of which is a criticism of what Kant calls "moral fanaticism." Kant regards as "self-conceit," "arrogance," "vain self-love," "a shallow high-flown, fantastic way of thinking" any incentive to morality other than "the thought of duty," which he would make "the supreme life-principle of all human morality."(CPrR, 87-88)

Kant has entered into the Christian Gospel to find support for his view. In the "Incentives" chapter of the "Analytic of Pure Practical Reason" he first mentions it when he is at his most persistent and even rhetorical expression of his view regarding the law of duty. ("Duty! thou sublime and mighty name that dost embrace nothing charming or insinuating but requirest submission. . . : what origin is there worthy of thee. . . ?") (CPrR, 89) Kant writes:

> The possibility of such a command as, "Love God above all and thy neighbor as thyself," agrees very well with this. [He has just said that we are subjects in the moral realm, not sovereigns, although legislative members

through freedom.] For, as a command, it requires respect for a law which orders love and does not leave it
to arbitrary choice to make love the principle. But to
love God as inclination (pathological love) is impossible,
for He is not an object of the senses.(CPrR, 85-86)

Kant then says that pathological love, or love through the
senses, is possible toward men, but that it cannot be commanded.
What Kant calls "that kernel of all laws," namely, the Gospel
injunction to love God above all and one's neighbor as oneself,
is practical love—to like to do His commandments, and to like
to practice all duties towards one's neighbor. All that is required by the command that makes this a rule is that we make
the effort to have this disposition.(CPrR, 86) "To command that
one do something gladly is self-contradictory."(CPrR, 86)

This first claim in the "Incentives" that Kant's moral philosophy and the teaching of the Gospel are in agreement moves
from his emphasis on duty to his emphasis on the disparity
between desires and inclinations and the moral law.

But the second reference in the "Incentives" to the Gospel is
found within the context of his discussion of moral fanaticism
as it bears upon his regard for the exclusive primacy of "intention." In the following quotation are found the fifth and sixth
references to "intention" in this first part of the "Incentives":

This reflection is not intended so much to clarify by
exact concepts the Gospel command [to love God, etc.]
just cited in order to prevent religious fanaticism with
reference to the love of God as to define accurately the
moral intention directly with regard to our duties to
others and to control and, if possible, to prevent a nar-
row moral fanaticism, which inflicts many persons. The
stage of morality on which man (and, so far as we know,
every rational creature) stands is respect for the moral
law. The disposition which obliges him to obey it is: to
obey it from duty and not from a spontaneous inclination or from an endeavor unbidden but gladly under-
taken. The moral condition which he can always be in is
virtue, i.e., moral disposition in conflict, and not holi-

ness in the supposed possession of perfect purity of the intentions of the will. (CPrR, 87)

Attention should be paid to Kant's explanation of virtue as "moral disposition in conflict." This concept of virtue seems to be the hinge by which his fear of what he calls "moral fanaticism" opens. He continues:

> The mind is disposed to nothing but blatant moral fanaticism and exaggerated self-conceit by exhortation to actions as noble, sublime, and magnanimous. By it people [85] are led to the illusion that the determining ground of their actions is not duty, i.e., respect for the law whose yoke must be borne whether liked or not (though it is a mild yoke, as imposed by reason). This law always humbles them when they follow (obey) it, but by this kind of exhortation they come to think that those actions are expected of them not because of duty but only because of their own bare merit. For not only do they not fulfill the spirit of the law when they imitate such acts on the basis of such a principle, since the spirit of the law lies in a submissive disposition and not in the merely lawful character of the act, leaving the principle to be what it may; and not only do they in this manner make the incentives pathological (locating them in sympathy or self-love) and not moral (located in the law); but they produce in this way a shallow, high-flown, fantastic way of thinking, flattering themselves with a spontaneous goodness of heart, needing neither spur nor bridle nor even command, to thereby forgetting their obligation, which they ought to think of rather than their merit.(CPrR, 87-88)

A brief review of the relationship of meanings among some crucial terms employed by Kant in the first part of Chapter III of the "Analytic of Pure Practical Reason," that is, in the chapter entitled "The Incentives of Pure Practical Reason," will reveal Kant's own "intention." The terms are the following: incentive, moral law, intention, duty, virtue.

An "incentive" is an "elater animi," a "lifting of spirit," a "motivation." The only "motivation" allowed is "intention" or "spirit," if the "moral law" is to be kept. Yet both the "spirit" ("intention") and the "letter" are required for the keeping of the "moral law." Thus "intention" is both *from* the "moral law" and directed *toward* the "moral law."

"Intention" is "reverence for the duty of the law." Nothing of what one would call "affective" or of what Kant calls "pathological," nothing from feeling or the senses, is to be included in Kant's moral thought. Love in the form of obedience and the effort to like the moral law is included. The success of the latter—liking the law—is in itself not reliable enough for Kant. This distrust seems to be related to Kant's explanation of "virtue" as "moral disposition in conflict." If conflict is present, the keeping of the "moral law" is not possible unless "duty" is invoked, and "duty" cannot be followed unless the "incentive" is "intention," which in turn is the indispensable requirement for keeping the "moral law."

Kant's "intention" in positing such an exclusive role for "intention" is to point to the perfection of the "moral law" itself. It is a claim that while it intends to "put in his place" the "created rational being," may exalt this "being" by maintaining that he can be moral without any help beyond his own created rational *will.* Thus while hoping to encourage humility and avoid self-flattery, Kant may have unwittingly encouraged the latter without aiding the former.

Henrik Ibsen's *The Wild Duck*[7] presents a character who has the intention of telling the truth. His name is Gregers Werle.

Act I is set at the home of Gregers's father, the older Werle, a wealthy businessman. A luncheon party is taking place in the dining room, and the conversation between two of the servants, Pettersen and Jensen, reveals that the older Werle has been a type of "ladies' man." The luncheon is for Gregers, who has been sent by his father to a branch of his business, what is known as "the Hoidal works."(TWD, 141)

From another room appears an old man by the name of Ekdal. He is shabbily dressed and somewhat unkempt. He is clearly not welcomed by Pettersen, the servant of the senior Werle. He wants to get into the office, which has a door to the right of the dining room. Pettersen tells him that the office closed an hour ago, but Ekdal says that Graaberg, the bookkeeper, is still there. Pettersen gives his consent but warns Ekdal, who goes in by the private door, "to go out the proper way."(TWD, 142)

Pettersen explains to Jensen that "old Ekdal" does some copying at home for the older Werle, when there is extra work to be done. He adds that Ekdal "had been a proper gentleman in his time," had been a lieutenant, gone into the timber trade, and, when Ekdal and Werle were running the Hoidal works together, Ekdal had played some kind of dirty trick on Werle, for which he had gotten either "penal servitude" or "first division." (TWD, 143)

As the host and guests leave the dining room, Werle points out to his son, Gregers, that there were thirteen of them at the table rather than the usual twelve. When Werle and guests leave the room, Gregers Werle and Hjalmar Ekdal, the son of old Ekdal, remain to talk.(TWD, 144)

Hjalmar has overheard the conversation, and says, "You shouldn't have sent me that invitation, Gregers."(TWD, 144)

Gregers replies, "What! The party is supposed to be for *me*. And if I can't ask my best and only friend—"(TWD, 144)

Gregers and Hjalmar are old schoolfellows and haven't seen each other in sixteen or seventeen years. Gregers asks Hjalmar how his father is, and Hjalmar tells him that his father now lives with him. Hjalmar begs off further discussion of his father—he says it is too painful—and asks how Gregers has been doing. In the conversation Gregers finds out that his father has discouraged contact with Hjalmar.(TWD, 144-46)

Hjalmar has taken up photography as a profession. His father's disgrace and lack of funds had forced him to discontinue his studies. Besides, there were debts, mostly to Gregers's father. Hjalmar tells that it was the older Werle who provided the money for him to study photography and to set up a studio. It was all supposed to be kept secret. It was also the older Werle who who made it possible for Hjalmar to marry. He asks if

Gregers knew about that. (TWD, 146-47)

Gregers answers:

> No, I certainly didn't. [Taking him by the arm and giving him a little shake.] But my dear Hjalmar, I can't tell you how glad I am about all this—but a bit bothered too. I may have been unjust to my father, after all, over certain things. Because all this shows a kind heart, doesn't it? It rather suggests the working of conscience— (TWD, 147)

Hjalmar asks, "Conscience?"(TWD, 147) Gregers brushes off the question and asks about Hjalmar's marriage. Hjalmar mentions his wife's name, Gina Hansen, and asks if Gregers remembers her, reminding him that she once kept house at the Werle's. Hjalmar tells Gregers that Gina worked there only a short time, in the last year of Gregers's mother's illness. Gina left either the year before Gregers's mother died or in the same year. Gregers says it was in the same year. (TWD, 147-48)

Hjalmar tells that Gina went to live with her mother, who also had a room to rent, which he took. Gregers's father had given him the idea. It ended in Hjalmar's and Gina's engagement. Then the older Werle helped him set up in business. It all worked out so well. Gina had even already had some lessons in retouching. (TWD, 148-49)

The other guests return, and Mrs. Sorby, the older Werle's housekeeper (whose relationship with Werle the servants Pettersen and Jensen had earlier conjectured about), dominates the conversation, bantering back and forth with several guests. (TWD,149-52)

Graaberg, the bookkeeper, looks in at the private door, saying he cannot get out, he is locked in, Flakstad's having gone off with the keys again. Werle says to come through where the guests are gathered, and although Graaberg warns that he is not alone, Werle says to come ahead, and Graaberg and old Ekdal emerge. Werle utters an involuntary "Ugh!" at the sight of Ekdal. (TWD, 152)

Hjalmar is of course surprised, but acts as if he did not notice who it was. He soon excuses himself from the party. (TWD, 152-54)

Gregers engages his father in a discussion of the Ekdal case, asking if Werle himself was not somehow implicated. Werle answers that Ekdal was condemned and he was acquitted, no matter how guilty or innocent Ekdal may have been. Werle tells his son that when Ekdal was released he was ruined. Nothing could be done for him.(TWD, 154-56) Werle says, "There are some people in this world who dive to the bottom the moment they're winged, and never come up again."(TWD, 156) Werle explains that he has gotten Ekdal the copying job and pays him far more than he's worth. (TWD, 156)

Gregers now confronts his father, questioning him on the financial records on the provisions made for old Ekdal, for Hjalmar, and presses him further about Gina Hansen, suggesting that Werle's relationship with her was more than that between employer and employee. Werle acts horrified that Hjalmar would be ungrateful enough to suggest such a thing, but Gregers says it was his own mother who told him shortly before her death. (TWD, 156-58)

Werle invites his son home and to a partnership in business. But the conversation reveals that Werle wants to marry Mrs. Sorby. Gregers tells his father that his friendliness and kind offer is for a selfish purpose. He wants to use Gregers to make the alliance with Mrs. Sorby socially acceptable. When Werle asks Gregers if this opposition has anything to do with his attachment to his dead mother, Gregers responds by saying that he is not neurotic. (TWD, 158-60)

It is at this point in the play that we see at least one view of Gregers's moral attitude made explicit. When Werle is trying to get Gregers on his side with regard to Mrs. Sorby's position, he says, "Doesn't it seem to you, Gregers—with your strong and definite views about justice—"(TWD, 160) Gregers seems to believe that he knows what justice is, or, at least, knows it and its opposite when he sees them.

Gregers blames his father's infidelities for his mother's mental condition. He sees his friend, Hjalmar, as victimized by his father's unscrupulousness. (TWD,161) Referring to Hjalmar, Gregers says:

> And there he is now, with his open, trustful, childlike mind, in the midst of all that deception, living under the same roof with a woman like that and never knowing that what he calls his home is built on a lie.(TWD, 161)

The older Werle and Gregers part ways but not before Gregers announces, "For now at last I see a purpose to live for."(TWD, 162)

Werle's comment: "And he says he's not neurotic." (TWD, 162)

Act I of *The Wild Duck* lines up all who by their own characters are capable of setting up others as victims of their own mind-sets.

Act II presents Gina, Hedvig, her child, and Hedvig's duck. Hjalmar returns from the luncheon but without bringing the good things he had told Hedvig he would bring. All he can offer her is the menu. Hjalmar has been disturbed by the events of the luncheon party, but is happy to be with Gina and Hedvig. Gregers Werle pays a visit, however. The older Ekdal shows him his simulation of the free and open life he once enjoyed in the timber business in the form of an attic inhabited by pigeons, hens, rabbits, and a wild duck—Hedvig's wild duck. Gregers learns that Hedvig has extremely poor eyesight.(TWD, 163-81)

It turns out that the older Werle, Haakon Werle, shot the duck, but only wounded it, so they have him to thank for this as well as for everything else! Old Werle has poor eyesight. The duck was only winged, dove to the bottom, and a dog of Haakon's rescued it. It was taken to Werle's house, Pettersen was going to kill it, and old Ekdal rescued it for his attic collection.(TWD, 182-83)

The Ekdals have a room to rent, and while Gregers is there he asks if he might have it. Gina tries to discourage him by telling him the room is really not adequate and that the two roomers right below him are rowdy and will disturb him. But he wants to come, says he is ashamed his name is Gregers Werle, and would rather be a clever dog.(TWD, 183-85)

Hjalmar sees the prospect of Gregers moving in as a good sign. He wants to "rise up" in life—no doubt to reassure himself that the father's misfortune is not fated to be the son's. He, too, has "a task in life," just as Gregers has found a "purpose." (TWD,186)

As Act III opens Hjalmar has invited Gregers as well as the two other roomers, Relling, a doctor, and Molvik, a former theology student, to lunch. After a conversation with Hjalmar about his work, Gina goes to the kitchen to prepare a herring salad. Hjalmar joins his father who is working on a new project in old Ekdal's attic. Hedvig is being allowed by her father to touch up the photograph he has been working on. Gregers Werle arrives. Gregers sits on the sofa and he and Hedvig are alone.(TWD, 188-93)

Gregers asks her about the wild duck, and she tells him all the things that she can look at and learn in the attic, where there are cupboards of books, many with large pictures in them. The duck comes up again and when Gregers says that the duck has been in "the ocean's depths," the phrase fascinates Hedvig such that she says that she might think of the attic as "the ocean's depths" if it weren't so silly, since, after all, it's only an attic.(TWD,194-97) Gregers asks, ". . . Do you know that for certain?"(TWD, 197)

Gina enters to set the table, and soon a shot is heard from the attic. Gina explains that Hjalmar and Ekdal go hunting in the attic. Gregers goes to the attic door. Hjalmar appears with a double-barrelled pistol. He puts it on the top shelf and warns Hedvig not to touch it since one of the barrels is loaded.(TWD, 197-99)

Gregers gets a good look at the wounded duck, and when Hjalmar and Hedvig explain why the duck drags one wing and is a little lame in one foot, Gregers, glancing at Hedvig, says, "—and has been in the ocean's depths—so long—".(TWD, 200)

Gregers and Hjalmar engage in conversation. Hjalmar confirms what Gina had earlier told Gregers. She does a good deal of the photography work to free Hjalmar for more important matters. Hjalmar is working on an invention.(TWD, 200) With reference to his taking up of photography, Hjalmar says:

> I swore that if I dedicated my powers to that craft, I would lift it to such heights that it would become both an art and a science, so I resolved to make this notable invention. (TWD, 201)

When questioned by Gregers as to the kind of invention he is working on, Hjalmar tells him not to ask for details, it takes time, and he is not doing it out of vanity or for his own sake. Rather it's the "purpose" of his life.(TWD, 201) Gregers inquires about Hjalmar's meaning and the latter says:

> Yes. I will rescue that ship-wrecked man. For he was ship-wrecked when the storm broke loose on him. By the time this terrible inquiry took place, he was no longer himself. That pistol there, my friend—the one we use to shoot rabbits with—it has played its part in the tragedy of the House of Ekdal.(TWD, 201)

Hjalmar relates that when the verdict was pronounced and his father was to go to prison, he had the pistol in his hand but had been broken into cowardice and was unable to use it. Hjalmar himself was so disgraced that he, too, had the pistol in his hand once, but "in that moment of supreme trial," he "won the victory" over himself. As Hjalmar has described that he felt as if the "whole creation should come to a stand, as in an eclipse" when his father was convicted, Gregers has said that he felt the same way when his mother died.(TWD, 202)

Gregers's moral temper is by now in full swing, and he begins to talk about poison in Hjalmar's house and about his own "purpose in life."(TWD, 204) When Relling and Molvik arrive for lunch(TWD, 205), and the talk gets around to Gregers, Relling asks, "And did you get that claim honoured that you were going around with?" Gregers knows what Relling means.

But Hjalmar asks, "Have *you* been taking up claims, Gregers?"

To Gregers's hedge Relling tells that "he went the round of the cottagers' huts and presented a thing called the claim of the ideal."

When Relling offers that perhaps Gregers has "enough sense

now to reduce the amount a little," Gregers responds, "Never, when I come upon a man that *is* a man."

As Hjalmar exchanges words of pride and affection with both Gina and Hedvig, who is to celebrate her birthday the following day, Gregers is unable to contain himself and says, "I, for my part, don't thrive on swamp vapour."(TWD, 206-208)

The hosts and guests respond as expected, but Relling accuses Gregers of bringing in the stench himself—from the mines. Relling says:

> Look here, young Mr.Werle, I have a strong suspicion that you're going about with the unabridged version of that "claim of the ideal" still in your pocket.(TWD, 209)

Gregers says that he carries it in his heart. Relling, aroused, threatens to throw him down the stairs if he brings out his "claim" there. Just when Hjalmar and Gina attempt their own interventions, the older Werle arrives asking for a private word with his son.(TWD,209-10)

Gregers tells his father that he intends to set Hjalmar right concerning the truth of things. The older Werle remonstrates with him, but Gregers appeals to his own conscience. Werle calls that conscience a "sick" one and leaves.(TWD, 210-12)

Hosts and guests return to the room, and Gregers asks Hjalmar to take a walk with him. When they leave Relling and Gina talk. Relling tells her that Gregers is "suffering from acute inflammation of the conscience." In answer to her question, Relling says that it is a disease, a national one, ". . .but it only breaks out sporadically." (TWD, 212-13)

When Hjalmar returns, his newly acquired knowledge, the "truth" that he now has, becomes the immediate cause of the catastrophe that begins its downward slide in Act IV.

All affection, all trust, is removed. He disdains the very thought of the attic and the duck, wants to take over the entire photography business himself, and decides to take over the bookkeeping from Gina. He even wants the duck killed but forbears to destroy it for Hedvig's sake. He has been fully indoctrinated by Gregers, but, of course, Hjalmar himself had evidenced some of the same moral temper earlier when he decided he had a "purpose" in life.(TWD, 215-16) Hjalmar now says:

> There are certain demands—what shall I call them?—
> suppose we say demands of the ideal, certain claims that
> a man cannot put aside without hurt to his soul.(TWD,
> 216)

Hjalmar persuades Hedvig to go out for her usual walk. He asks Gina what was between her and the older Werle. Gina says that nothing occurred until after Werle's wife died and she had returned to her home. Hjalmar cannot understand why Gina's conscience has not been wracked with remorse during the fifteen years of their marriage. He resents having lived in what he calls a "swamp of deceit."(TWD, 217-20) He says it is "all over."(TWD, 221)

Gregers Werle returns, disappointed that the couple shows no sign of "the transfiguring light of understanding." (TWD, 221) Gregers had hoped that Hjalmar's "great enlightenment" would have been "an initiation to something higher."(TWD, 222) He says to Hjalmar, "For surely no experience in life can equal the forgiving of a sinner, lifting her up by your love to stand beside you?"(TWD, 222)

Relling comes in. Mrs. Sorby arrives on the scene, announcing that she and Werle will marry. She leaves and Hedvig returns saying that as they passed in the doorway, Mrs. Sorby gave her a letter addressed to "Miss Hedvig Ekdal." It is Haakon Werle's handwriting. Hjalmar opens it. It is deed of gift, first, to the older Ekdal—no more copy work at the office and five pounds every month. After his death the five pounds a month go to Hedvig—five pounds a month for the rest of her life.(TWD, 222-33)

Hjalmar confronts Gina. Is Hedvig Werle's child or his? She says she does not know. She is angry and defiant. Hjalmar answers, "Then I have nothing more to do in this house." (TWD, 234)

Gregers says, ". . .You three must be together if you are to win the great sacrament of forgiveness." (TWD, 234) But Hjalmar says he has no child and Hedvig's "No, no! Don t go away from me!" does not deter him.(TWD, 234)

Gregers: "You do believe, Mrs. Ekdal, that I meant it all for the best?

Gina: "Yes, I half believe you did; but God forgive you, all the same."(TWD, 235)

Relling had earlier warned that certain upsets are extremely dangerous for someone of Hedvig's age, an adolescent. Now Hedvig begins to suspect that Hjalmar is not her father. She muses that he was very fond of her anyway. She says she prays for the wild duck and for Hjalmar, too, every night. (TWD, 236)

Gregers has engaged Hedvig in conversation and suggests that Hedvig sacrifice the wild duck for Hjalmar's sake. It is the most precious thing that she has and would be a perfect sacrifice. Hedvig says that she will ask her grandfather to shoot the wild duck for her—but in the morning. Gregers tells her to keep it secret from her mother.(TWD, 237)

Act V takes the turn of events in the play to the bottom. Hjalmar has been out on the town with Relling and Molvik. Gregers continues to talk of Hjalmar's need for "solitude," his "conflict of spirit," "spiritual upheaval," his "personality," "innermost being." Relling is trying to take care of everybody for all are "sick," he says. The cure he prescribes is "the saving lie," which, he says, is "the stimulating principle of life." He tells Gregers to stop using "that exotic word 'ideals'," and to employ rather the "good enough native word: 'lies'."(TWD, 240-44)

Gregers, however, considers Relling a bad influence on Hjalmar. Relling's philosophy: "Take the saving lie away from the average man, and you take his happiness away, too." (TWD, 244)

Hedvig, having slept on the idea, does not think it very good to shoot the wild duck. But she does ask her grandfather what one would do if one were to shoot a wild duck—not hers, just any wild duck. He says that it would have to be shot in the breast and *against* the lie of the feathers, not *with* the feathers.(TWD, 244-45)

Hedvig then goes to the bookcase, stretches up to the top shelf, takes the double-barrelled pistol down, looks at it, and puts it down when her mother comes in from the living room. Hjalmar returns, he and Gina argue over how bad he looks, and Hedvig, seeing him, shouts for joy, "Oh, Daddy! Daddy!"(TWD, 246)

Hjalmar turns away and says, "Go away! Go away! Make her go away from me, I tell you." (TWD, 246) He gets ready to leave again, but wants his books since he needs them for his invention, and intends to take his father with him. Gina tries to give him some hot coffee, bread and butter, and salt meat, but he wants his notes for his autobiography, his diary, his important papers. He opens the living room door and pulls back, saying, "There she is again!"(TWD, 247-48)

Hedvig hears him say, "In the last moments I spend in my former home I wish to be spared contact with things which are not my concern," and running toward her mother she asks, "Is that me?"(TWD, 248)

As Hjalmar tries to get his things together, he looks for his loaded pistol. It is gone and Gina supposes that old Ekdal has taken it into the attic with him. Meanwhile, Hjalmar is feeling sorry for himself, drinking the coffee, and looking for the butter for his bread. He is sitting on the sofa, and he asks Gina if he would be left unbothered by anybody were he to put up in the living room for a day or two. He is stalling. He has earlier picked up Werle's letter with the notice of the legacy, and he again turns it over, saying that although he has no intention of doing anything with it, it should not be lost.(TWD, 249-51)

Gregers Werle reappears. Hjalmar reveals that it was Relling who first told him that he was capable of getting an invention out of his photography skills. But it was Hedvig's belief in it that had kept him going, kept him working on it. (TWD, 252-53)

Hjalmar speaks of his love for Hedvig. He says that he built up the illusion that she was as devoted to him as he was to her. When he came home, she flew to meet him. He tells Gregers that he suffers from the terrible doubt that Hedvig never really loved him at all. (TWD, 253-54)

A pistol shot is heard. Gregers explains that Hedvig has gotten her grandfather to shoot the wild duck to prove her love for her father, to win back his love, since she does not think that she can live without his love. (TWD, 255-56)

"Hedvig, come along! Come in here to me!" This is Hjalmar's answer to her sacrifice for him. (TWD, 256)

But Hedvig does not come. Old Ekdal does. Realizing that it was not his father who fired the shot, Hjalmar rushes to the door of the attic, opens it, looks in, and screams, "Hedvig!" (TWD, 257)

Relling is called. The bullet has entered the breast.

"Ah, Thou above! If Thou art here! Why hast Thou done this thing to me!" Thus Hjalmar shrieks to heaven. (TWD, 258)

When he turns to Gina to ask if she can bear it, she says that now they "have equal shares in her." (TWD, 259)

Gregers is horror-stricken, his face is twitching, and he cannot figure out how such a thing could have happened. He says, "Hedvig has not died in vain. Did you see how sorrow called out what was noblest in him?" (TWD, 259)

But Relling says, "Before the year is out little Hedwig will be nothing more to him than a fine subject to declaim on."(TWD, 259)

When Gregers says that if Relling is right and he is wrong then life is not worth living, Relling answers that life would be "tolerable enough . . . if we could only be rid of these infernal duns who come to us poor people's doors with their claim of the ideal." (TWD, 260)

Gregers: "In that case, I am glad my destiny is what it is."

Relling: "May I ask—what is your destiny?"

Gregers: "To be thirteenth at table."

Relling: "I wonder. . . ." (TWD, 260)

Gregers Werle believes in telling the truth. He has what he thinks is a good intention, and he would judge himself to be obeying another requirement that Kant attaches to morality: the categorical imperative. Of the several expressions of this Kantian requirement, Gregers could in good conscience say that his actions conform to all of them. Yet some would call him a dangerous busybody.

Dr. Relling believes that his moderate approach to moral

thinking and acting is the right one. Yet some would call him a cynic, or super-rational.

The kind of love that exists between Hedvig and Hjalmar would be called pathological by Kant, and thus as having nothing positive to do with morality. Certainly the other loves—that between Hjalmar Ekdal and Gina, Haakon Werle and Gina, Gregers Werle and his mother, Haakon Werle and Mrs. Sorby, Hjalmar Ekdal and his father—would fare no better in Kant's distinction between (1) pathological or "sensible" love and (2) "liking" the moral law, or trying to "like" it, or doing one's duty.

The difficulty resides in the assessment of psychological motivation. Not even Kant could know all of his own motivations. It is true that a moral agent cannot be held as accountable if he is unaware of why he does what he does, but that does not make the action performed wholly moral. There is more to morality than intention.

Kant knew that there was; he was only trying to emphasize that for an action to pass the "categorical imperative" test, it had to be done *from* duty.

Was it Gregers's "duty" to inform Hjalmar that Gina had had relations with Werle before her marriage to Hjalmar?

Kant says that reason does not by its nature necessarily conform to the objective law. Because of this fact, the only incentive must be the moral law. The question remains: what *is* the moral law?

In *Foundations of the Metaphysics of Morals* Kant writes:

> [Thus the first proposition of morality is that to have moral worth an action must be done from duty.] The second proposition is: An action done from duty does not have its moral worth in the purpose which is to be achieved through it but in the maxim by which it is determined.
>
> The third principle, as a consequence of the two preceding, I would express as follows: Duty is the necessity of an action done from respect for the law.[8]

In this same work, when Kant is explaining why duty must be the basis of morality, he says that to be truthful from duty is different from being truthful out of fear of consequences. (J, 197)

> The shortest but most infallible way to find the answer to the question as to whether a deceitful promise is consistent with duty is to ask myself: Would I be content that my maxim (of extricating myself from difficulty by a false promise) should hold as a universal law for myself as well as for others? (J, 198)

Kant then tells what an *imperative* is. It is the formula of a command of reason which is itself the conception of an objective principle, so far as it constrains a will. Imperatives are either hypothetical or categorical. The hypothetical has to do with means to ends. The categorical is one that presents an action as of itself objectively necessary, without regard to any other end.(J, 199) The categorical imperative is the imperative of morality.

Kant says:

> The imperative thus says what action possible to me would be good, and it presents the practical rule in relation to a will which does not forthwith perform an action simply because it is good, in part because the subject does not always know the action is good and in part (when it does know it) because his maxims can still be opposed to the objective principles of practical reason. (J, 200)

It is this possibility of the subject's maxims being in opposition to the objective principles of practical reason that makes the emphasis on intention so problematic.

Kant writes, "What is essentially good in it [the categorical imperative] consists in the intention, the result being what it may."(J, 201)

Kant states the categorical imperative after he has said that there is "only one categorical imperative": "Act only according to that maxim by which you can at the same time will that it should become a universal law. . . ."(J, 204) Kant says that the imperative is "an a priori synthetical practical proposition. . . ." (J, 203) He adds an explanatory footnote:

> I connect a priori the will, without a presupposed condition resulting from an inclination, with the action (though I do so only objectively, i.e., under the idea of a reason which would have complete power over all subjective motives). This is, therefore, a practical proposition which does not analytically derive the willing of an action from some other volition already presupposed (for we do not have such a perfect will); it rather connects it directly with the concept of the will of a rational being as something which is not contained within it. (J, footnote, 203)

Thus Kant takes into account the imperfection of every human will, and prior to any experience of any human individual will, from which he does not think we can get a *law*, he simply connects the willing of an action with the concept of the will of a rational being. The categorical imperative works only on the assumption that the human will is rational, even while it admits that will's imperfection. The moral law is perfect, and reason has reliability—if it knows its limits. The only thing good without qualification is a good will. (J, 191) Yet that will is the will of a rational being.

Kant's emphasis on will (intention) to the neglect of the act itself, the circumstances, and the consequences has its appeal. In the reading Kant always appears morally rigorous. He does provide a caution against moral fanaticism like that of Gregers Werle, and against the cynicism of Relling. He is a corrective, as is Relling, for a false idealism in his observations on the imperfections of human willing. But Kant's emphasis on intention can produce another fanaticism, moral subjectivism or moral relativism—in spite of his own intentions. His view of the morality that can be reached by the universalizing into law of what one has in mind to do as a test of the moral worth of the action gives man a sovereignty which Kant at the same time denies that he has. He has said that the "created rational being" is a subject in the moral realm, not a sovereign. But he has also said that the "created rational being" is a legislator in the moral realm, one who cannot be holy, but can be moral. This kind of reductionism or minimalism can serve as a corrective to human pride. It can also make the "created rational being" arrogant before his Creator, unwilling to see even his own moral efforts as dependent on God.

Notes

1. *Encyclopedia of Philosophy*, Reprint Edition, s.v. "Kant, Immanuel."
2. Ibid.
3. Ibid.
4. Ibid.
5. Ibid.
6. Immanuel Kant, *Critique of Practical Reason*. All further references to this work will be cited in the text as *CPrR*.
7. Henrik Ibsen, *The Wild Duck*, trans. Una Ellis-Permor, 1950. All further references to this play will be cited as TWD.
8. Kant, *Foundations of the Metaphysics of Morals*, in Johnson, pp.190-209. All further references to this work of Kant's will be cited from the Johnson text as J.

Bibliography*

Suggested Readings

Collins, James. *A History of Modern European Philosophy*. Lanham, Maryland: University Press of America, 1953.

Copleston, Frederick, S.J. *A History of Philosophy*, Volume 6, Parts I-II. Garden City, New York: Doubleday & Co., Inc., Image Books, 1964.

Green, Ronald M. *Religion and Moral Reason*. New York: Oxford University Press, 1988.

Ibsen, Henrik. *Hedda Gabler and Other Plays*. Trans. Una Ellis-Fermor. New York: Penguin Books, 1950.

Kant, Immanuel. *Critique of Practical Reason*. Trans. Lewis Beck White. New York: Macmillan Publishing Co., 1956.

——————— . *Critique of Pure Reason.* Trans. Norman Kemp Smith. New York: St. Martin's Press, 1965.

——————— . *Foundations of the Metaphysics of Morals.* Trans. Lewis Beck White. Indianapolis: Bobbs-Merrill Co., Inc., 1959.

Murphy, Jeffrie G. and Jean Hampton. *Forgiveness and Mercy.* Cambridge: University Press, 1988.

* Kant is difficult to read. The list of his works far outnumbers the three above. Yet to read these, which are primary, would be a challenge. Other works can be found listed in "Kant," *The Encyclopedia of Philosophy,* Reprint Edition, cited above under "Notes."

V

SCHELER
PERSON IS PRIMARY

Max Scheler was born in Munich in 1874. An emotional man, and one of great learning, he was also characterized by his love of new experiences. His father's family, traced to the sixteenth century, was a family of jurists and Protestant clergymen. His mother was Jewish. Religious conflict was a theme throughout Scheler's life. Scheler was baptized in his teens, and returned to the practice of the Catholic faith in 1912.[1]

Scheler's early philosophical career was greatly influenced by Rudolf Eucken, an idealist and liberal. In 1901 Scheler became *Privatdozent* at the University of Jena. In 1907 he moved to the University of Munich and his own thinking began to take shape. He met several disciples of Husserl there [and then went on to Gottingen where he met Husserl himself.] Scheler turned to the phenomenological movement. By 1910 Scheler had retired from teaching, and had begun to live as an independent writer in Berlin.[2]

The move to Berlin marked the second and most fruitful period of Scheler's life. Here he wrote either the drafts or final versions of some of his most important work: *On Resentment and Moral Value Judgments*, 1912; *Contributions to the Phenomenology and Theory of Sympathy and of Love and Hate*, 1913; *Formalism in Ethics and Non-Formal Ethics of Values*, 1913-1916. At the outbreak of World War I, he wrote *The Genius of War and the German War*, 1915, a glorification of German involvement in war. During 1917 and 1918 he carried out diplomatic missions in Geneva for the German Foreign Office.[3]

By 1920 Scheler had shifted his political ground. He wrote *On the Eternal in Man* in 1921. After the war, he held the chair of philosophy and sociology at the University of Cologne and wrote *Contributions to Sociology and to the Study of World Views, 1923-1924,* which became *Forms of Knowledge and Society, 1926.*[4]

Four years before his death, Scheler entered the third period of his life. He turned from Catholicism and from theism, moving toward a comprehensive anthropology close to vitalism and pantheism. His interest had in part moved to the natural sciences. Out of this development came *The Place of Man in the Universe,* 1928, and *Man in the Age of Equalization,* 1929. He had gone to the University of Frankfurt early in 1928, where he died in the same year.[5]

Max Scheler's entire ethics is a statement as to the priority of personal values over all non-personal values. In Part II, Chapter 6, Section B, Number 1, of *Formalism in Ethics and Non-Formal Ethics of Values,* Scheler treats of "The Nature of the Moral Person." He elaborates on four conditions for personhood: (1) a wholly sound mind; (2) a certain level of development; (3) domination over the lived body; (4) distinction from "soul-substance" and "character."[6]

The person is the unity of being of his acts.(FENEV, 383) Yet these acts do not cover the idea of person because the person also transcends his acts.[7] The limits within which beings are to be taken as persons has never been set "by man simply as man."(FENEV, 476) Scheler maintains nevertheless that the concept of person is applicable only to a specific level of human existence.(FENEV, 478-79)

Scheler emphasizes "understanding" in the first condition for being a person: 1) a wholly sound mind.(FENEV, 476-78) The fourth condition: 4) distinction [of person] from "soul-substance" and "character" achieves an even fuller description of the moral person.(FENEV,482-89) Finally, the second and third conditions: 2) a certain level of development(FENEV, 478-79); 3) domination over the lived body, complete the description. (FENEV, 479-82)

Since Scheler devotes more space to condition #1 and condition #4, these may be treated first. Conditions #2 and #3 will follow.

A Wholly Sound Mind

1) By a wholly sound mind Scheler means soundness in the phenomenological sense, not in the positive, scientific sense. A phenomenologically sound mind is one that tries to "understand" the expressions of someone else rather than to explain them "causally." Such a mind does not deny that psychic processes take place and that they have causes, but the fact of psychic processes is never present as a state of affairs.(FENEV, 476-77)

For "understanding" it is necessary to experience, out of the "spiritual center" of the other, the acts of the person: speech, expressions, and deeds. These acts are experienced as intentionally directed toward something by the other. The being who is a person, who is of sound mind, re-executes the acts of the other, re-judges his spoken statements and the corresponding judgments. The sound of mind re-feel the other's feelings, re-live his acts of will. To all of this is attributed some sense.(FENEV, 477)

Two things follow from the above. (1) Psychological objectification is depersonalization. (2) The person is one who executes intentional acts that are bound by a unity of sense. Psychic being has nothing to do with personal being.(FENEV, 478) Person is primary, preceding his psychological profile.

Soul-substance and Character

4) The primacy of the person is manifest in Scheler's attempt to distinguish between person and character, and person and soul-substance.(FENEV, 482-89) Soul-substance is thought of as a real *object* consisting of hypothetically attributed properties, forces, faculties, dispositions, etc. Thus experiential contents of the individual ego can be causally explained in terms of changing conditions of real effects of stimuli on the "soul." But person

is the concrete "subject" of all acts of the essence of inner intuition, in which everything psychic becomes objective. The person as *subject* experiences psychic states as *objects*. Thus the person is not only never an object, but never a real *thing*, either; he "is" only as "the concrete unity of acts executed by the person. . . ."(FENEV, 482-83) The person experiences but is never experienced.(FENEV, 482-83)

Neither is the person the same as character. Character is taken as the enduring dispositions of the will or other dispositions—of the mind, intellect, memory. But the action of the person is not merely the consequences of these dispositions. The person and his actions freely vary, even with no change in disposition of soul, body, or situations.(FENEV, 484)

Dispositions of character require causal (biological and historical) explanation. Facts such as conversion become explicable in terms of "change in character." A new explanation is required for the new fact.(FENEV, 484-85)

In the cognitive relation to another person, the individuality of the person can be understood from a single action and from any phenomenal expression of that person.(FENEV, 485) Moreover, another's deeds can be ethically measured, not only by moral laws, but also by the intentions of the person himself.(FENEV, 485) Of great importance for ethics is the differentiation of concepts like "morally good," "psychologically normal," "morally bad," "pathological"; distinguishing between person and character makes the differentiation possible.(FENEV, 485)

Accountability and Responsibility

The person stands behind psychological change. Such change may make him "invisible" to others because of illness, and judgment about his person may become impossible. Nevertheless, we assume the existence of the person behind the changes. Thus we attribute "imputability" to his actions although we do not say he is "responsible" in specific aberrations. Psychological illness nullifies the "imputability" of the actions with regard to his person, but it does not nullify the responsibility of the person in general.(FENEV, 485-86)

Responsibility is essentially connected with the being of the person. Imputability or accountability nullifying this responsibility implies that the effectiveness of "motives" deviates from the normal effectiveness of these motives. It is thus impossible to decide whether a given action belongs to the person of the man.(FENEV, 486)

Every person remains responsible for his personal acts. Responsibility is a presupposition of accountability, not the other way around, which would be deterministic.(FENEV, 486)

To say that someone is accountable is to say that his actions can be coordinated with acts of his person. Unaccountability denies this possibility. It does not deny responsibility, simply the determination of responsibility for certain actions. Both concepts—accountability and unaccountability are formed from the outside.(FENEV, 486-87)

Moral responsibility is not so formed. Here the person experiences himself as "responsible" in his reflection on an action as his action. Not only are actions included in this experiencing, but also "acts of the moral tenor, potential moral tenors, intentions, things done on purpose, wishes, etc."(FENEV, 487)

This experience of responsibility, although it is reflective, is not so in any sense other than that of the person's immediately knowing that he is the author of a deed.

> The concept of moral responsibility has its roots in one's immediately knowing that he is the author of his deed and its moral value-relevance, not in any subsequent connection in thought of an executed and completed act or action with the self. The experience of *"self-responsibility"* as an absolute experience is the presupposition of all responsibility "before" someone (man, God), i.e., of all relative responsibility.(FENEV, 487)

It cannot be said the the person is ill or healthy, only that the man or the soul is ill or healthy.(FENEV, 487)

> One who fails to see the essence of the person, as all psychologistic (and vitalistic) ethics does, must come to

86

the conclusion that there is no essential difference between "morally evil" and "sick," between evil and "ata-
vism" or lower stages of development.(FENEV, 487)

Love of the Person

The factual person and his life-expressions and actions can be
measured by the value-intentions immanent to the person himself, by his own ideal value-essence, and not only by general
moral norms. Such measurement would not be possible if the
person were known "inferentially," as the cause of these expressions, etc. It is character that is known in this inferential
way.(FENEV, 487)

In fact, we morally assess another by

> the ideal picture that we form by bringing to their end
> ... the *basic intentions* of the other person which have
> been obtained through a central understanding of his
> individual *essence* and which we unite with the concrete
> ideal value-picture of the person given only in
> intuition.(FENEV, 488)

How is this intuition of the person's ideal and individual
value-essence reached? It is reached through the understanding
of his most central source. How is that reached? It is reached
through love of the person.(FENEV, 488)

The empirical, historical, and psychological knowledge of a
person's life conceals his essence. No induction can determine
his essence. Yet the intuition of the person's essence is never
complete, either. But it is the condition of any full understanding of his actions and expressions.(FENEV, 488)

> All psychology—even so-called differential psychology—
> secures its object only by abstracting from and disre-
> garding the person. Hence the person is totally transcen-
> dent to psychology. What psychology yields, even in
> ideally perfect fashion, is merely possible material of the
> person's life that can be structured in one way or
> another.(FENEV, 488-89)

The two middle conditions for being a person advance Scheler's thought on moral responsibility: 2) a certain level of development, and 3) domination over the lived body.

A Certain Level of Development

2) Scheler holds that this level of development, this maturity, consists at its most basic level in the ability to have insight into the difference between one's own and someone else's acts, willing, feeling, thinking.(FENEV, 478) Someone is immature as long as he wills what parents, educators, and others want him to do without recognizing in his willing the will of a person different from himself.[8] Thus he takes an "alien" will for his "own," and his "own" for the "alien" one.(FENEV, 479)

When the others whose will, feelings, and thinking the immature person has taken on are present, he can differentiate from them only by reason of such willing, etc., coming from their bodies. He is not able to tell the difference between his own acts, etc., in recollection, when the others who are really doing his willing, thinking, feeling for him are not bodily present.(FENEV,479)

It is in the insight into the difference between one's own acts and another's, not in the ability to understand all the distinctions operative in Scheler's philosophy of person—in particular, as his philosophy outlines maturity—that a being "comes of age." Scheler writes:

> For this reason I say that the essence of maturity lies in the immediate *being-able*-to-differentiate and in the immediate consciousness of the ability to differentiate, not in the factual possession of distinctions. We can say that it lies in "the genuine being-able-to-understand." (FENEV, 479)

Domination over the Lived Body

3)Scheler's third requirement for being a person is domination over the lived body. One who lives predominantly *in* his lived body is not a person. The person does not identify himself with the contents of his lived body. The person experiences his lived body—identifying it in inner and outer perception—as belonging to himself. The lived body is the "original" property of the person, and only by this being the case can he have any other property, such as inanimate things.(FENEV,479-80)

Promising is a good criterion for deciding whether or not a human being is master of his lived body. In order to promise, there must be continuity between willing and being-able-to-do. Such willing and its continuation in being-able-to-do is in principle independent of the states of the lived body.(FENEV, 480-81)

Scheler considers promising a natural not an artificial act.

> For "promising" is not an "artificial" act based on convention, as psychologism (for example, Hume's) teaches; that is, it is not simply an act having the content "I will do this if you will do that" (and vice versa) so that a contract becomes the root and foundation of this act (and not a consequence of it).(FENEV, 481)

Scheler holds that slaves, and to some extent, women, are not able to fulfill this requirement of being a person—domination over the lived body. They cannot maintain the continuity between willing and being-able-to-do. This view of Scheler's is partly attributable to the social and legal circumstances of the historical period in which he lived. Nevertheless, he seems to believe that some are "slaves" by reason of factors other than positive law.(FENEV, 480-81)[9] Scheler notes that Christianity recognizes "a religious personal nature in women" and that "women can be holy, too," but he points out that such recognition exists only in private law and not in state or public law. These philosophical/historical positions are used by Scheler to buttress his argument that person is not the same as ego or soul.(FENEV, 481-82) He writes:

> These facts show that the very idea of the person has nothing to do with the ideas of the ego and the soul and analogous concepts in ethical and legal domains. Just as there can be ego-being and soul (including the human soul) without any personality (in the strict sense), it

makes perfect sense to assume a personality where there is neither ego nor soul (for example, when we speak of the person of God, who can confront neither an outer world nor a "thou").(FENEV, 482)

Walker Percy's *The Second Coming* is a novel about people who exhibit varieties of sanity and insanity, love and lovelessness.[10] As the novel proceeds, Percy seems to be trying to present two people who by finding each other somehow lose a world from which they *should* be alienated. Will Barrett, lawyer, the hero (or, if you will, anti-hero), is a Southern gentleman (North Carolina), middle-aged, a widower of a Northern (New York) and moneyed "good" if unattractive woman (a Peabody). Will is first seen on the golf course and then headed to his far-better-than-average Southern house with its five-car garage. Will is not in good health. He keeps falling and he can't keep his mind on the everyday. He thinks a good deal about God, the state of religious belief in the U.S., and about his and others' sexual life.

In a contemplative mood, with Luger in hand as he sits in his garage, he experiences a rifle shot from a nearby forest that ends up in the inner wall of the garage, and a bee sting.

> Later he remembered thinking even as he dove for cover: Was not the shock expected after all? Is this not in fact the very nature of the times, a kind of penultimate quiet, a minatory ordinariness of mid-afternoon, a concealed dread and expectation which, only after the shot is fired, we knew had been there all along?
>
> Are we afraid quiet afternoons will be interrupted by gunfire? Or do we hope they will? (TSC, 15-16)

Will has a revelation, which he likens for its smiling certitude to Einstein's insight as the latter boarded a Zurich streetcar. Will looks at his cat and sees that it is one hundred percent cat. People are not like that. Einstein was three hundred percent himself, some are forty-seven percent themselves, and all too many just two percent themselves.

> How can the great suck of self ever hope to be a fat cat dozing in the sun?(TSC, 16)

The shot had come from Ewell McBee, new Southerner and poacher, who has long been in Will's life as the "poor white antagonist."

Allie Huger is the heroine. Allie is about the same age as Will's only child, daughter Leslie. Allie is also the daughter of old flame Kitty Vaught. But Allie has been institutionalized. She escapes from Valleyhead Sanatorium in a bread van. She has to write notes to herself because of memory deficit from being "buzzed" (ECT—electroconvulsive therapy) so much.

> From the pocket of her jacket she took out the red spiral-bound notebook and opened it. At the top of the first page was written in blue ink and in her hand the following:
> Date: October 15
> Place: Room 212, Closed Wing, Valleyhead Sanatorium
> Below, printed in capital letters and underlined, was the following:
> INSTRUCTIONS FROM MYSELF TO MYSELF
> What followed was written in her ordinary script: As I write this to you, I don't remember everything but I remember more than you will remember when you read this. You remember nothing now, do you? I know this from experience. Electroshock knocks out memory for a while. I don't feel bad. To tell the truth, I'm not even sure I'm sick. But they think I'm worse because I refuse to talk in group (because there is nothing to say) and won't eat with others, preferring to sit under the table (because a circle of knees is more interesting than a circle of faces).(TSC, 26-27)

Allie has made it to Linwood, checked in to Mitchell's Triple-A motel, and after some beauty shop work, and a few purchases, she goes to claim the property she remembers that her Aunt Sally left her. It ends up being no more than a greenhouse. She sets up housekeeping, and on one fine day, Will Barrett's golf balls intrude.

"Are these yours?"

. . . .
"Yes. Spalding Pro Flite and Hogan four.
Yes, that's them all right. Thanks."(TSC,74-75)

Thus begins a romance that appears to be a statement about contemporary man (and woman), authenticity, second chances and second "comings"—Will had not been "in love" with his first wife, Marion, but had married her apparently because she had wanted him to marry her and he had wanted to make her happy! Kitty, who in his youth had looked very good to him, now is an emblem of the contemporary scene in which neither he nor Allie can find spiritual space. They find space in a Holiday Inn eventually, and promise to love forever. Will is still the heir of his Mississippi and Georgia memories and is still caught up in his questions about God. He hopes the clergy, in the person of old Father Weatherbee, will tell him what to believe.

> "Tell me something, Father. Do you believe that Christ will come again and that in fact there are certain unmistakable signs of his coming in these very times?"(TSC, 359-60)

But the novel ends with the priest giving Will no answers. Instead, Will finds his own.

> Will Barrett thought about Allie in her greenhouse, her wide gray eyes, her lean muscled boy's arms, her strong quick hands. His heart leaped with a secret joy. What is it I want from her and him, he wondered, not only want but must have? Is she a gift and therefore a sign of a giver? Could it be that the Lord is here, masquerading behind this simple silly holy face? Am I crazy to want both, her and Him? No, not want, must have. And will have. (TSC, 360)

Scheler's "person" and Percy's two main characters can profitably be compared. Will and Allie are presented as two people who might have trouble passing the tests of clinical psychologists, but do pass Scheler's test for soundness of mind. At least they take each other at face value without probing for causes of behavior. They may not take others in the same simple, accepting way, but they seem to offer to one another what Scheler describes as "understanding."

Their ethics does not pass the "character" test, but they do act from the "spiritual center" that is the core of Scheler's "person." Will manifests concern for his "soul" that does not seem to separate it from his "person," however.

Issues of immorality as distinguished from insanity arise in the novel, and issues of accountability as distinguished from responsibility also are prominent. Allie is not "normal"; she is not thought to be "responsible" enough to function outside a sanatorium, and yet she has to "give an account" of herself through the sanatorium's group meetings and has to undergo electroshock in order to improve her behavior. Clearly, Percy asks throughout the novel the question, Who is sane, Allie or her parents? Is Dr. Duk sane? His answer: Will and Allie are more moral and they act more responsibly than do the other characters. It is in their "difference" from the shallow people that surround them that they are seen as "persons."

Percy may want their maturity (sufficient "level of development") to be seen as reached in their finding of each other, and acceptance of each other. This interpretation may be the best one. Human love is divine, or all we can be sure of without risking illusion.

The last lines of the novel (quoted above) leave room for a less benign interpretation. Will and Allie are no different at the end of the novel from the twentieth century man Will Barrett criticizes early in *The Second Coming*. To run away from the "great suck of self" they have each become one hundred percent "fat cat dozing in the sun" of the greenhouse. Something else is needed to convert the sucking self.

> (God plus any creature) cannot be conceived as greater than God alone.

> (God plus any creature) cannot be conceived as better than God alone.[11]

93

Is the great impasse the error—the gravest of errors—that God is "one of us" in a sense that sins against the First Commandment? Is this an Age of Idolatry?[12]

Notes

1. *Encyclopedia of Philosophy*, Reprint Edition, s.v. "Scheler, Max."
2. Ibid.
3. Ibid.
4. Ibid.
5. Ibid.
6. Max Scheler, *Formalism in Ethics and Non-Formal Ethics Values*, 476-489. All further references to this work will be cited in the text as FENEV.
7. Karol Wojtyla, now Pope John Paul II, has studied Scheler deeply. Between the two philosophers there are points of agreement and disagreement. In Wojtyla's *The Acting Person* the relationship between spirituality and transcendence is articulated in the following way:

> ... the evidence of the spiritual nature of man stems in the first place from the experience of the person's transcendence in the action. ...(TAP, 181)

Wojtyla understands "the person's transcendence in action" as accounted for in "the essential surrender of the will to truth."(TAP,138) He also points out that a certain "transcendence" is one in which "... the subject confirms himself by transgressing (and in a way outgrowing) himself."(TAP, 309, n.41.) In the same place Wojtyla attributes this meaning of transcendence to Kant not Scheler. Such transcendence "... is not ... directed toward an object (value or end). ..."(TAP, 309, n.41) It is not a transcendence "toward truth."(TAP, 310, n.48)
8. Scheler's idea of person is opposed to the view that what many would count as persons, for example, embryos and infants, are persons. Questions in medical ethics are unfortunately often answered with a view like Scheler's.
9. Scheler says that "... the place ... in which the nature of the person first flashes before us is to be sought only in a certain *kind* of man, not in man in general—a kind, that is, which varies considerably in its

94

positive historical delineation."(FENEV, 476) By itself, this statement leaves room for all men and for all women to realize personhood. Scheler says that "children or imbeciles" might be said to have the "seeds of personhood."(FENEV, 476) Nevertheless, until all reach Scheler's four requirements, they are not considered to be persons.

10. Walker Percy, *The Second Coming,* 1980. All further references to this novel will be cited in the text as TSC.

11. See Robert Sokolowski, *The God of Faith and Reason,* 7-9. Sokolowski says that these statements are implicit premises in St. Anselm's argument for the existence of God in Chapter Two, Three, and Five of the *Proslogion.* ("God is that than which nothing greater can be thought," being the explicit premise in Chapter Two, and "God is that than which nothing better can be thought," in Chapters Three and Five. The argument proceeds: But it is greater (better) to exist in reality than in the mind only. Thus if God is that than which nothing greater (better) can be conceived, He must have existence in reality as well as in the mind. Therefore, God exists.)

12. Manfred Frings in *Max Scheler,* 1965, quotes Scheler's *On Eternal in Man:* "Every finite spirit (Geist) believes either in a God or an idol."(OEM, German Edition, 261)

Bibliography

Suggested Readings

Frings, Manfred S. *Max Scheler.* Pittsburgh, Pennsylvania: Duquesne University Press. Editions E. Nauwelaerts, Louvain, 1965.

Gretlund, Jan Nordby and Karl-Heinz Westarp, eds. *Walker Percy: Novelist and Philosopher.* Jackson: University Press of Mississippi, 1991.

Percy, Walker. *The Second Coming.* New York: Farrar, Straus and Giroux, 1980.

_____ . *Signposts in a Strange Land,* ed., with an introduction by Patrick Samway. New York: Farrar, Straus and Giroux, 1991.

Scheler, Max. *Formalism in Ethics and Non-Formal Ethics of Values,* trans. Manfred S. Frings and Roger L. Funk. Evanston: Northwestern University Press, 1973.

Sokolowski, Robert. *The God of Faith and Reason.* Notre Dame, Indiana:

University of Notre Dame Press, 1982.

Wojtyla, Karol (Pope John Paul II). *The Acting Person*, trans. Andrzej Potocki and ed. Anna-Teresa Tymieniecka. Boston: D. Reidel Publishing Co., Analecta Husserliana, Vol. X, 1979.

Works by Scheler in English Translation *

On the Eternal in Man, trans. Bernard Noble. London: SCM Press, 1960.

Man's Place in Nature, trans. and with an introduction by Hans Meyerhoff. New York: Noonday, 1961.

"Metaphysics and Art," trans. Manfred Frings. In *Max Scheler: Centennial Essays*. The Hague: Martinus Nijhoff, 1974.

The Nature of Sympathy, trans. Peter Heath, with an introduction by W. Stark. Hamden, Conn.: Archon Books, 1970.

Philosophical Perspectives, trans. Oscar Haac. Boston: Beacon Press, 1958.

"Problems of a Sociology of Knowledge," trans. Ernest Ranly. *Philosophy Today*, Vol. XII, no. 4 (Spring, 1968), pp. 4270.

Ressentiment, trans. William Holdheim, with an introduction by the editor, Lewis A. Coser. Glencoe, Ill.: Free Press, 1961.

Selected Philosophical Essays, trans. and with an introduction by David R. Lachterman. Evanston, Ill.: Northwestern University Press, 1973.

"On the Tragic," trans. Bernard Stambler. *Cross Currents*, Vol. IV (1954), pp. 178-91.

* From "Bibliography" in FENEV, 602.

VI

MARCEL
COMMUNION IS REAL

Gabriel Marcel was born in Paris, December 7, 1889, and died on October 8, 1973. His father was at one time French minister to Stockholm. Marcel benefited from a multilingual milieu and from extensive foreign travel. During World War I he worked with the Red Cross, responding to the inquiries of families about loved ones missing in action, an exposure to the realities of human existence. After this experience the inability of abstract thought to comprehend the drama of human existence was imprinted on his mind and emotions.[1]

Marcel's philosophy is nonacademic, even though he took the *agrégation* in philosophy from the Sorbonne at the age of twenty. He taught only intermittently. Marcel was a prolific and award-winning playwright, a music and drama critic for leading French journals, and an accomplished pianist. The profoundly integral nature of his thought was such that he ranked music as one of the most important influences on his philosophy. Marcel became a Catholic in 1929.[2]

Although generally classed among the existentialists—and considered a foremost Christian existentialist—Marcel himself did not like the designation. He is scarcely influenced by Kierkegaard, and his philosophy was worked out before other twentieth century existentialists, such as Heidegger, Jaspers, and Sartre.[3]

Marcel's "On the Ontological Mystery"[4] continues his project of describing the human being and his existence, even anticipating that the earthly experience will have its consummation elsewhere. (OTOM, 46) The work explores themes that dominate Marcel's thought. One such theme is that of communion.[5]

Sanctity and Philosophy

Marcel maintains that the topic of sanctity is one for philosophical speculation, and indeed one that would be the best starting point for a new ontology. He writes:

> But it is, above all, the sanctity realised in certain beings which reveals to us that what we call the normal order is, from a higher point of view, from the standpoint of a soul rooted in ontological mystery, merely the subversion of an order which is its opposite. In this connection, the study of sanctity with all its concrete attributes seems to me to offer an immense speculative value; indeed, I am not far from saying that it is the true introduction to ontology.(OTOM, 42)

Ontology or metaphysics, the study of what is, of the "really real," or of being as being, has traditionally made the distinction between the one and the many the basic distinction. Marcel prefers a distinction between the full and the empty as more fundamental.(OTOM, 12) If sanctity is to be the subject of speculation for a new ontology, this preferred distinction may help. We speak of holiness as fullness, as, for example, when we say, "Hail Mary, full of grace."

Intimacy, Availability, Presence

Communion is intimacy. *Co-esse*, genuine intimacy, *being with*, is all the higher and secured the more that it is grounded in the realm of total spiritual availability (*disponibilité*), pure charity. In so far as *being with* another is on this plane, it is communion.(OTOM, 39) The deeper such communion is, the closer it approaches to the real.

Communion is also presence. The test of presence is death. A being who has been granted to us as a presence is a being to whom we will keep present through creative fidelity. We do not carefully preserve this being in effigy as we would an object. Creative fidelity is ontological in principle. It prolongs presence which is a kind of hold on us.(OTOM,36-37)

Fidelity and Hope

Faithfulness is the opposite of conformism. Faithfulness recognizes the permanent, not as one recognizes a law, formally. Rather faithfulness recognizes the permanent, ontologically. Fidelity is so far from conformism that it requires an interior struggle to avoid the dissipation of the ideals once embraced, and against the hardening that is the negative aspect of habit. Fidelity to be creative is not fidelity to a principle. Fidelity does not prolong principle; it prolongs presence.(OTOM, 35-36)

Hope implies credit, whereas despair implies complete insolvency. Hope asserts that at the heart of reality, of being, the mysterious is in connivance with me—and this beyond the data, inventories, and calculations that are set before me.(OTOM, 27-28) Mistrust is appropriate in the scientific laboratory, but not in the inquiry concerning the value of life. It is the mind chained to objectivity that sees in all contexts mistrust as appropriate and event as problem.(OTOM, 27-30)

Hope is not passive waiting, nor does it spring from pride.(OTOM, 32) Marcel writes, "Could not hope therefore be defined as the will when it is made to bear on what does not depend on itself?"(OTOM, 33)

> The experimental proof of this connection is that it is the most active saints who carry hope to its highest degree; this would be inconceivable if hope were simply an inactive state of soul. The mistake so often made here comes from a stoical representation of the will as a stiffening of the soul, whereas it is on the contrary relaxation and creation.(OTOM, 33)

The withdrawal in recollection, the humble pulling back, as distinguished from the proud contraction and self-removal, is of the essence of hope that is creative, and of fidelity that is creative.(OTOM, 34)

Mystery and Problem

Ontology, what is taken to be the study of being, of all that is, is not a problem to be solved. It is rather in its beginning and in its end and indeed throughout a mystery. "A mystery is a problem which encroaches upon its own data, invading them, as it were, and thereby transcending itself as a simple problem." (OTOM, 19)[6]

Some examples: the mystery of the union of body and soul; the mystery of evil. To regard these as problems we act as if we are God and God uninvolved, God as onlooker. On the contrary we are involved in both of these. We are body/soul. We are touched by evil.(OTOM, 19-20)

It is in love that the frontier between problem and mystery is best seen as obliterated. We cannot really say what love is because we have a criteriology only for the order of the objective and the problematical, but love does not belong to these— it is not to be reduced to will to live, will to power, or *libido*.(OTOM, 20)

We have encounters that we could reduce to the explicable, the coincidental, the might-not-have-been. But we are *inside* these encounters, and they develop from within us. Such meetings have acted on us as inward principles. We are in the presence of mystery.(OTOM, 21-22)

Mystery is not less real for not being able to be fully grasped by the mind. Communion itself is heavily freighted with mystery. Why is this person my intimate? Why is this other one a saint? Empirical data, the essence of "problems" and their "solutions," are not adequate to the questions. Yet the intimacy and the sanctity are nonetheless real.

Loss of the sense of being, or a failure in awareness of it is the condition of modern man. Marcel questions whether a deeper psychoanalytical method might "reveal the morbid repression of this sense."(OTOM,10) It could be that the impossibility of placing being under a microscope, or of anaesthetizing it on the operating table, or of computing it, or, indeed, of making profit from it, has lulled modern man to unconsciousness of being.

Function in the System

Marcel notes that once in a while a poem or a piece in a periodical may reflect on the wonder of simply *being*. Most of the time the concern is over *doing*, in the sense of performance for its own sake or for the sake of production or profit or prestige. Thus it is that what one does is taken for what is real, and the first question often is "What do you do?" What is your function in the system?[7]

In our age the individual thinks of himself as a collection of functions, a collection perhaps without any stable ranking of the functions. When the vital or physical functions are considered, the concept of man is restricted by historical materialism and Freudian doctrines. When the social functions are considered, man becomes the consumer, the producer, the citizen. On the subway, for example, there is the man who opens the doors, the one who punches the tickets. Everything is so arranged that the man is taken to be no more than his functions. His social and vital functions become conflated. He lives on a "time table." (OTOM, 10-11)

> So many hours for each function. Sleep too is a function which must be discharged so that the other functions may be exercised in their turn. The same with pleasure, with relaxation; it is logical that the weekly allowance of recreation should be determined by an expert on hygiene; recreation is a psycho-organic function which must not be neglected any more than, for instance, sex.(OTOM, 11)

Details vary, but there is a vital schedule. Disorder enters with illness and accidents, and the smooth running of the system gives way.(OTOM, 11)

> It is therefore natural that the individual should be overhauled at regular intervals like a watch (this is done in America). The hospital plays the part of the inspection bench or the repair shop. And it is from this same standpoint of function that such essential problems as birth control will be examined.(OTOM, 11)

Death is "the scrapping of what has ceased to be of use and must be written off as total loss."(OTOM, 11-12)

A functionalized world is a sad one; the man who has retired from his work presents a dreary picture, and, indeed, is granted mere tolerance.(OTOM, 12)

To try to leave out mystery, as the functionalist world does in the face of birth, love, and death, is ". . . to bring into play . . . that psychological and pseudo-scientific category of the 'purely natural'."(OTOM, 12-13) At work in this thinking is ". . . the remains of a degraded rationalism from whose standpoint cause explains effect and accounts for it exhaustively."(OTOM, 13)

The Ontological Need

Marcel claims there is an "ontological need." We do inhabit a world with an infinite number of problems calling for research into causes. Problems are both theoretical and technical, these being interdependent, and solutions have to be found so that the various functions can work together without doing harm to one another.(OTOM,13) Marcel says that "...the ontological need, the need of being, is exhausted in exact proportion to the breaking up of personality . . . and . . . the triumph of the category of the 'purely natural'. . . ." (OTOM, 13) The consequence is the "atrophy of the faculty of *wonder*." (OTOM, 13)[8]

What is this ontological need? First, it is never completely clear to itself. But Marcel tries a description.(OTOM, 13)

> Being is—or should be—necessary. It is impossible that everything should be reduced to a play of successive appearances which are inconsistent with each other ("inconsistent" is essential), or, in the words of Shakespeare, to "a tale told by an idiot." I aspire to participate in this being, in this reality—and perhaps this aspiration is already a degree of participation, however rudimentary.(OTOM, 14)

Marcel offers, not a definition of being, but "a method of approach."(OTOM,14) ". . . being is what withstands—or what would withstand—an exhaustive analysis bearing on the data of experience and aiming to reduce them step by step to elements increasingly devoid of intrinsic or significant value."(OTOM, 14) Philosophy can and does reject such a need.(OTOM, 14)

The ontological need is not only indeterminate in character; it is also paradoxical. When we ask questions concerning being, we, the questioners, are not outside of the being we question.(OTOM, 15-16) It is only by a "fiction that Idealism in its traditional form seeks to maintain on the margin of being the consciousness which asserts it or denies it."(OTOM, 16-17)

We want to make an affirmation regarding being, yet it is not until it is made that we are qualified to make it.(OTOM, 17) The investigator thinks, and as he thinks he is not exactly affirming anything; he keeps up the thinking, even to an infinite regress; yet it is he who recognizes the regress and thus in some sense transcends it. This process takes place within an affirmation of being, an affirmation which the thinker *is* rather than *says*.(OTOM, 17-18)

The inquirer into being assumes an affirmation in regard to which he is in some sense passive. This occurs only at the extreme limit of thought, which limit the thinker cannot reach without falling into contradiction. He thus assumes or recognizes a form of participation which is the subject not the object of thought. This participation cannot serve as a solution; it is beyond the realm of problem-solution; it is meta-problematical.(OTOM, 17-18)

Conversely, if the meta-problematical can be asserted, it has to be thought of as transcending the opposition between the subject who asserts the existence of being and being as asserted by the subject. The meta-problematical must be seen as underlying this opposition between "subject" and "being." But to posit the meta-problematical is to posit the primacy of being over knowledge, not of being as asserted but of being as asserting itself. To posit the metaproblematical is to recognize that knowledge is environed by being.(OTOM,18)

> . . . contrary to what epistemology seeks vainly to establish, there exists well and truly a mystery of cognition; knowledge is contingent on a participation in being for

which no epistemology can account because it continually presupposes it. (OTOM, 18)

Marcel asks if there is any help for this condition. His answer is affirmative. Detachment from experience is necessary. Detachment is only accomplished in recollection. One's initial reflection postulates the ontological, but without knowing it. Second reflection asks how and by what starting point one is able to proceed in first reflection. Second reflection is recollection to the extent that recollection can be self-conscious.(OTOM, 23-25)[9]

Communion, involvement, participation in being are real. An ontology that is sound would begin with the saint because in the saint these are fully *realized*. The saint is detached from experience, recollected. The saint recollects, and the re-collection is not a summing up of experience but a transcending of it through mystery. For the saint *being* is before *knowing*. Thus access to a new ontology is through the saint and the saintly attributes.

That communion is real, that participation is not optional, is the burden of Marcel's argument. What grounds the argument is anticipation of a different order from that of nature and of reason.(OTOM, 46) Looking forward to "the life that is to come" is warrant against suicide, and against life without mystery.

Karol Wojtyla has written a play entitled "The Jeweler's Shop."[10] The subtitle reads: A Meditation on the Sacrament of Matrimony, Passing on Occasion into a Drama.

Perhaps the first indication of the seriousness of the subtitle is found in the opening speeches, first of Teresa, and then of Andrew. The reminiscence of the evening of Andrew's "proposal" supports the view that what comes from God, specifically from the Holy Spirit, is above all peaceful. His emblem is the dove. Teresa says in the first speech of the play:

> He didn't say, Do you want to be my wife
> but "my life's companion."
>
> I answered yes—not at once

but after a few minutes,
and yet in the course of those few minutes there was no
need for reflection, no need to struggle between motives. The answer had almost been determined. We
both knew that it reached deep into the past and
advanced far into the future,(TJS,279)

Andrew's first speech shows how he knew that Teresa was
right for him.
... I don't think I even know what "love at first sight"
means.
After a time I realized she had come into the focus of my
attention—
I mean I *had* to be interested in her,
and at the same time I *accepted* the fact that I had to.(TJS,
280)

His assent, however, is related to an act of the will. Other
women have charmed him. Beauty accessible to the senses has
attracted him. But having noticed that such beauty can cause
those led by it to hurt others, he has come to appreciate the
beauty accessible to the mind—truth. He had wanted to regard
love as passion, had believed in the absolute of emotion. He
says:
And that is why I could not grasp
the basis of that strange persistence of Teresa in me,
the cause of her presence,
the assurance of her place in my ego,
or what creates around her
that strange resonance, that feeling "you ought to."(TJS,
281)

One October evening Teresa and Andrew stop in front of a
jeweler's shop. They look at the rings in the window. These will
mark their fate, act as a reminder of the past, a lesson to be
memorized once and for all, and they will open up the future,
join past to future. And they are for all time, too.(TJS, 286)

105

Someone speaks loudly behind their backs:
> This is the jeweler's shop. What a strange craft
> to produce objects that can
> stimulate reflection on fate,
> to gild watches, for instance, that measure time and tell
> man about the transience of all things and their
> passing.(TJS, 287)

The window of the jeweler's shop functions in the play as present and literal mirror, but also as a mirror of reminiscence and one that projects images of the future.

But now they enter the shop and get measured for their rings. And again the future—at their wedding—where the sparkling wine becomes an image of the radiation of each into the other's life. Yet "... man will not endure in man forever,/ and man will not suffice."(TJS, 292)

The jeweler's shop window reflects them, but it is no ordinary flat mirror that just reflects; it also absorbs them. Andrew says, "I had an impression of being seen and recognized by someone hiding inside the shop window."(TJS, 292) Teresa says that she had the impression that their reflection had been there, could not be removed.(TJS, 292) So goes Act I of Wojtyla's meditation. Wojtyla has entitled this act "The Signals."

In the month of August that preceded the month of Andrew's "proposal," the month of October, they had been hiking with a large group of close friends in the mountains, when they all heard a call, like a wailing, or groan, or whine. It could have been a man, or a bird. The call was repeated and the boys called back. No response came. For Teresa the experience evoked the thought of signals and on the evening of Andrew's "proposal," she again thinks of signals—this time about signals that cannot connect—just as the signals on the mountain two months before had not connected. Andrew is not able to reach her depth, yet knows that she is his focus on the way to maturity.(TJS, 282-84)

In an exchange of letters between the two, we see that Teresa says that on that mountain night she saw Andrew as he was—one who tries "to calculate...happiness at any price," as he calculates in his planning office, one who lacks courage and trust in life, his own fate, people, God. Andrew's letter tells Teresa that her courage, her reaching for happiness, is "only another form of fear—or caution, at least."(TJS, 288)

Through the words of the jeweler as he tests the fineness of the metal of the wedding rings that Teresa and Andrew will purchase, Wojtyla underlines the brevity and yet the seriousness of each human life. Referring to the "weight" of the human being, the jeweler says:

> It is the weight of constant gravity
> riveted to a short flight.(TJS, 289)

Act II presents a different couple, Anna and Stephan, and its title is "The Bridegroom." Anna's first speech is about the rift between her and Stephan. Anna remembers the jeweler's shop as it was to her when their love was "indisputable."(TJS, 295-96) She decides she might as well sell her ring back to the jeweler now—Stephan will probably not even notice its being gone, such is his indifference. (TJS,297)

When the jeweler attempts to weigh the ring, he tells her:

> ... "This ring does not weigh anything;
> the needle does not move from zero,
> and I cannot make it show
> even a milligram.
> Your husband must be alive,
> in which case neither of your rings, taken separately,
> will weigh anything—only both together will
> register."(TJS, 297-98)

Anna and Stephan, with three children from their union, have nonetheless fallen away from love. She tells her story to the "chance interlocutor" whom she meets on the one day she has tried to return to the jeweler's shop, only to find it closed. From the first return, when the jeweler had weighed her wedding ring and found it wanting, she had deliberately taken a different route home. The interlocutor's name is Adam.(TJS, 298-99)

Anna later remembers Adam's words: "Here is the jeweler's shop again; soon the Bridegroom will pass by." (TJS, 299) By these words Adam means that as the Bridegroom passes, he touches the love that is in people. If the love is bad—and it is only bad when there is a lack of it—the Bridegroom suffers. Adam tells Anna that when one wants to run away from one's life, one really needs to return to it instead.(TJS,299-300) Adam says:

> "... Life is an adventure,
> and at the same time it has its logic
> and consistency—
> that is why one must not leave thought
> and imagination on their own!"
> "With what is thought to remain, then?" Anna asked.
> It is to remain with truth, of course.(TJS, 300)

But Anna thinks that what one feels the most strongly is the truth. To her, love is of the senses; two people are united by feeling. Not quite, says Adam. "Love is ... a synthesis of two people's existence,/which converges ... at a certain point/and makes them into one."(TJS, 300)

Anna now wants a different, a younger man—to try again. She meets four men, and after the fourth one, who invites her to join him, and to whom she responds, comes the touch of a fifth man's hand—Adam's. He says, "No."(TJS, 300-304) Adam shows Anna the street, where they see four girls with lamps on their way to buy some oil. Adam tells Anna that the fifth girl is missing, that these four are the wise virgins. He also points out to her the foolish virgins, who are sleepwalkers. He says:

> They are walking in a lethargy—they have a dormant space in them. You now feel that space in you, because you too were falling asleep. I have come to wake you. I think I am in time.(TJS, 305)

Adam tells her that the Bridegroom is always waiting—on the "... far side of all those different loves without which man cannot live."(TJS, 305)

As they continue their walk, Anna sees a man with Stephan's face; she hates the face she ought to love. Adam explains that when we look in the Bridegroom's face, we see the faces of all

108

of those with whom love has entangled us in our lives; they are all in him.(TJS, 308)

Anna rouses herself from her meditations and is in front of the jeweler's shop again. It is again shut but she feels the jeweler's gaze and hears his words:

> "You must never be below the level of my sight;
> you must not fall lower, for the weight of your life
> must be shown on my scales."(TJS, 308)

Act III, "The Children," reveals that the child of Teresa and Andrew, Christopher, and a child of Anna and Stephan, Monica, are in love. Christopher was last held in the arms of his father, Andrew, at two years old, when Andrew told Teresa and their son good-by before going to war. The couple's love remains only in the child—Andrew was killed at the front.(TJS, 309-10)

Teresa speaks interiorly to the dead Andrew, telling him how the two of them, and also Anna and Stephan, weigh upon the fate of Monica and Christopher. Both couples have suffered a rift, but the cause is different. Teresa still wears Andrew's ring and he died with hers on his finger, and Anna and Stephan do not wear theirs.(TJS, 313-14)

Monica and Christopher visit the jeweler's shop, and Teresa at first cannot understand why their experience is not like the one she has in her memory of her own and Andrew's visit. At Monica and Christopher's wedding Adam takes Andrew's place. He had "been with him at the front." It is not that he is interested in Teresa for marriage, but only that since every man's previous fate has its roots in him, so must every man's future fate.(TJS, 317-18)

The play ends with a reconciliation between Anna and Stephan. After meeting Adam, Anna starts looking at her own failings and she and Stephan become less burdensome to one another until they decide to split the guilt between them.

Adam reflects:

> Sometimes human existence seems too short for love.
> At other times it is, however, the other way around:
> human love seems too short in relation to existence—or
> rather too trivial. (TJS, 321)

He says that all people have available an existence and a love. They have to build out of these a structure that makes sense, one that must never be inward-looking. It must be open to embrace other people, but also reflect the absolute Existence and Love.(TJS, 321)

The last words spoken by Teresa in the play are the following:

> Ah, the jeweler has locked up his shop.
> And the two young people have both gone away.
> Do they know at least what they reflect?
> Should one not follow them?
> But after all, they have their own thoughts. . . .
> They will come back here; they will certainly come back.
> They have simply gone to ponder for a while:
> to create something, to reflect the absolute Existence and
>   Love,
> must be the most wonderful of all!
>
> But one lives in ignorance of it.(TJS, 321-22)

"The Jeweler's Shop" dramatically echoes "On the Ontological Mystery"—not deliberately, but because it is about being or existence, which neither work takes to be merely human. "The Jeweler's Shop" is explicit about existence's origin, dependence, and end, and yet, as a literary work, much is done by way of implication. "On the Ontological Mystery," as a philosophical piece, is expected to be explicit, yet its religious nuances remain implicit.[11] Together these attest to the fact that if ethics is to be a practical discipline, it cannot be devoid of sound idea nor of concrete expression.

Communion is real. Union with God from whom we came is always left intact in some way. Not even the lost are without missing Him. His presence is ineluctable. All communion between one human being and another is ontologically related to the communion between God and each. The Bridegroom always waits to be noticed.

Questions of holiness, presence, intimacy, fidelity, hope, problem, mystery, death can be understood only in light of the human being's participation in the life of God.

Human love, and, in particular, marital love, has to remain under the Eye of God. The following brief reference to Pope John Paul II's address for the tenth anniversary of the John Paul II Institute for Studies on Marriage and the Family will say what should be said and lived:

> The Church, conscious of its own inalienable duty to promote and defend the divine plan for the conjugal sacrament, proclaims unceasingly that *consilium Dei* [not *consilium hominis*] *de matrimonio et familia,* which can and must always be recognized as a *gift of God* to humanity.[12]

It is divine counsel, not mere human counsel, that is a gift of the Spirit.

Notes

1. *New Catholic Encyclopedia,* 1967, s.v. "Existentialism," 736a-b.
2. Ibid.
3. Ibid.
4. Marcel, "On the Ontological Mystery," in *The Philosophy of Existentialism,* 9-46. All further references to this work are cited in the text as OTOM.
5. The word "communion" has powerful religious connotation for those who have religious faith, but also for those who do not. In *Existentialism from Dostoevsky to Sartre,* Walter Kaufmann writes that he has omitted Marcel (and Berdyaev, Buber, Bultmann, Tillich) from his book because religion has always been existentialist. It is just that now existentialist concerns have entered philosophy; Marcel was influenced by Jaspers, whom he does include (and Bultmann by Heidegger, Tillich by Schelling), and none of those excluded "has so far left a mark, like Kierkegaard, on literature or on philosophy"; existentialism can be accounted for without reference to the religious existentialists, while those who know existentialism can better understand what the religious existentialists are saying. See Kaufmann, 49-50.

6. Copleston in *Contemporary Philosophy* begins his discussion of Marcel with the latter's distinction between problem and mystery.

> A "problem" is a question which can be considered purely objectively, a question in which the being of the questioner is not involved. A mathematical problem is a case in point.

> A "mystery" on the other hand is a question which involves the being of the questioner, so that in considering the question or theme the questioner cannot disregard himself.(Copleston, 166)

To explain what Marcel means by "mystery," Copleston uses the question "What am I?" As physiologist I can answer the question by making it a "problem," but if I want the question to answer more, and "I" am part of the question, something escapes analysis. The question then turns from "problem" to "mystery." Copleston notes that "mystery" in Marcel is neither revealed truth nor the unknown. It refers to what is given in experience but cannot be objectified in a way in which the subject is disregarded.(Copleston, 166-67)

7. In *Existentialism* John Macquarrie writes in reference to Marcel's criticism of "functional man":

> Functional man, reduced to a factor in the empirical social reality, is deprived of mystery, dignity, personhood, and eventually of humanity itself.(Macquarrie, 176)

Macquarrie quotes Marcel's *Man Against Mass Society*: "The dynamic element in my philosophy, taken as a whole, can be seen as an obstinate and untiring battle against the spirit of abstraction."(MAMS, 1)

8. It is heartening to see the efforts of *Handbook of Metaphysics and Ontology*, edited by Burkhardt and Smith, 1991. The Preface reads:

> This somewhat pleonastic title reflects the different histories of the terms metaphysics and ontology in the two cultures of Anglo-Saxon and Continental philosophy. On the one hand the term metaphysics has pejorative overtones in continental philosophy as a result of the still pervasive influence of Kant's critique. On the other hand the term ontology has an honourable history, above all in German philosophy from Goclenius and Wolff to Husserl and Ingarden, and both terms are employed ever more frequently in the writings of the more sophisticated analytic philosophers in ways which to

some degree reflect an effort to build bridges to the classical metaphysical tradition.

9. Copleston explains "first reflection" and "second reflection" by noting that when one person loves another and then analyzes it by some criteria, perhaps, Freudian, there is "first reflection." Objectification, problem, and first reflection go together. In "second reflection" there is an attempt on the part of the person loving to love and reflect on his or her love in one and the same act. The reflection is from within the experience itself. Second reflection and mystery go together.(Copleston, 167-68)
10. Wojtyla, "The Jeweler's Shop," in *The Collected Plays and Writings on Theater*, 277-322. All further references to this play appear in the text as TJS.
11. Marcel of course is also a playwright. See Bibliography below.
12. Address of His Holiness Pope John Paul II on the Occasion of the Tenth Anniversary of the Establishment of the John Paul II Institute for Studies on Marriage and the Family, March 23, 1992, 2-3.

Bibliography

Suggested Readings

Copleston, Frederick. *Contemporary Philosophy*. Revised Edition. New York, New York: Newman Press, 1972.

Macquarrie, John. *Existentialism*. Reprint Edition. New York, New York: Penguin Books, 1982.

Marcel, Gabriel. *The Philosophy of Existentialism*, trans. Manya Harari. Secaucus, N.J.: Citadel Press, 1956.

Wojtyla, Karol. *The Collected Plays and Writings on Theater*, trans. Boleslaw Taborski with introductions. Berkeley: University of California Press, 1987.

Works by Marcel *

Philosophical works

Journal métaphysique. Paris, 1927. Translated by Bernard Wall as *Metaphysical Journal*. Chicago, 1952.

Être et avoir. Paris, 1935. Translated by Katharine Farrar as *Being and Having*. London, 1949.

Du Refus à l'invocation. Paris, 1940. Translated by Robert Rosthal as *Creative Fidelity*. New York, 1964.

Homo Viator. Paris, 1945. Translated by Emma Craufurd. New York, 1962.

The Philosophy of Existence. Translated by Manya Harari, New York, 1949. Republished as *Philosophy of Existentialism*. New York, 1961.

Le Mystère de l'être, 2 vols. Paris, 1951. Translated by G. S. Fraser and René Hauge as *The Mystery of Being*, 2 vols. Chicago, 1950.

Hommes contre l'humain. Paris, 1951. Translated by G. S. Fraser as *Men Against Humanity*. London, 1952. Republished as *Man Against Mass Society*. Chicago, 1962.

L'Homme problématique. Paris, 1955.

Présence et immortalité. Paris, 1959.

The Existential Background of Human Dignity. Cambridge, Mass., 1963.

Plays

"The Lantern," *Cross Currents*, Vol. 8, No. 2 (1958), 129-143.

Three Plays, translated by Rosalind Heywood and Marjorie Gabain. New York, 1958; 2d ed., 1965. Contains "A Man of God," "Ariadne," (*Le Chemin de Crête*), and "The Funeral Pyre" (*La Chapelle ardente*; in the 2d ed., "The Votive Candle").

---

* *Encyclopedia of Philosophy*, Reprint Edition, s.v. "Marcel, Gabriel."

VII

LEVINAS
TRANSCENDENCE IS SELF-LESS

Emmanuel Levinas was born in Kovno, Lithuania, in 1906, into a Jewish family. Jewish influences were present in his childhood and early youth. In fact, these were more than simply "influences." Other cultures also exercised their strong pull. His parents knew Yiddish, yet Russian was also spoken at home. In school he developed a love for the Russian classics, which he says awakened his philosophical interests.[1]

In 1923, at the age of seventeen, Levinas went to France to study at the University of Strasbourg. During the following decades, non-Jewish interests engrossed him. He became especially interested in the thought of Husserl and Heidegger, both of whom he studied with in 1928-1929 at the University of Freiburg. Levinas's career in the French intellectual world reached its peak with his appointment as professor of philosophy at the Sorbonne in 1973. Levinas had previously taught at Poitiers and Nanterre, and enjoyed many and frequent contacts with the great figures of French intellectual life.[2]

The Other

Levinas's ethics is an ethics of "the other." It is an ethics of transcendence. Transcendence is "desire for the Good beyond being."[3] As creatures we are bonded to the Good, but we are unable to attain the object of our desire. In the bond with the Good there arises both vulnerability to others and responsibility for others.

Three essays by Levinas, if taken together, can be seen as

providing a foundation for his emphasis on alterity. They are "Humanism and An-archy," "No Identity," and "God and Philosophy."[4] Transcendence, as "desire for the Good beyond being," with vulnerability and responsibility for others, is selfless. Creatureliness defines subjectivity. Creatures are possessed by the Good. They are not their own.

Subjectivity and Responsibility

Levinas locates our subjectivity in our bond with the Good, in our bond with God.[5] The Good took possession of the subject before the subject had the chance to choose. This Good commands us.[6] This Good is so good that subjection to it, obedience to it, is obedience to a value that has no anti-value; the name is God.(HA, 136)

Passivity

For Levinas subjectivity is radical passivity. Subjectivity is passive in its root; we are profoundly passive to God. God acts on us—more than that, our subjectivity is defined by dependence on God, our Creator.

The Good dominates the subject. The subject (you, and I, and all the others) is elected; it does not elect or choose. Such election by the Good is *so non-violent that it is not even an action.* [Italics mine.] Being elected is a "passivity more passive than any passivity."(HA, 135)

Levinas says that subjectivity is prior to the ego, prior to consciousness. With the ego arises disobedience and irresponsibility. Subjectivity is an inwardness that is ineffable and incommunicable.

We have this deep and wordless bond with the Good, and yet what we find around us are the others, and these others are the ones to whom we must respond. Subjectivity, then, is described as responsibility for others.(HA, 132-33)

Levinas's project of redescribing the subject was motivated by the events of history; specifically, by the events, the atrocities, against human beings during World War II. Levinas understood that the last several centuries preceding the present one had valued a humanism that had not worked out very well in terms of the lives and well-being of human beings. This humanism had been essentially without God. Human reason had attempted to supplant God, but all its progress—and the progress had been real and praiseworthy—had not kept men from destroying one another.(HA, 127)

Levinas, along with other post-World War II intellectuals, saw that such high-spirited humanism, deriving ultimately from Enlightenment optimism, had not helped those who were bombed, gassed, and incinerated in the name of progress.

Vulnerability

Levinas takes up the theme of vulnerability—the human ability to be wounded—as he re-describes subjectivity. Noting that for the sciences of man everything human is outside, "everything in me is open," Levinas asks, "Is it certain that in this exposedness to all winds subjectivity is lost among the things or in matter? Does not subjectivity signify (have meaning) precisely by its incapacity to shut itself up from the outside?"[7]

Levinas then recognizes the several senses of openness: first, the openness of every object to all others; second, the intentionality (purposefulness) of consciousness founded in the truth of being (is-ness) or being's essence; third, "openness is the denuding of the skin exposed to wounds and outrage."(NI, 145-46)

Subjectivity signifies in its incapacity to cut off the outside. Subjectivity is "a radical passivity of man, who ... declares himself to be, and considers his sensibility an attribute."(NI, 146)

Levinas asks the interesting question, "*Is* it?" *Is* vulnerability? He has said that this sensibility which is vulnerability is before "will, action, declaration, all taking up of positions."(NI, 146) Then in asking if this sensibility, this vulnerability *is*, he asks if perhaps the *being* of vulnerability does not "consist in divesting itself of being, not in dying, but in *altering* itself (literally, "othering" itself), in otherwise than being."(NI, 146) Levinas is speaking of "giving," of "serving," especially at a loss to one-self, to the extent that he wonders if vulnerability can be said to *be*, if rather it is more like *non*-being.(NI, 146)

This "relationship with the other" which is vulnerability is not a matter of being affected by the other as by a cause. The other is not just the other who stimulates me to suffer. Vulnerability is an "aptitude . . . 'to be beaten,' 'to receive blows,'" and Levinas quotes Lamentations 3: 30: "He offered his cheek to the smiters and was filled with shame."(NI,146)

Although in sensibility the subject is *"for the other:* there is substitution, responsibility, expiation,"(NI, 147) yet this responsibility is passive, prior to freedom. "The passivity of the vulnerable one is the condition (or uncondition) by which a being shows itself to be a creature." (NI, 147)

The Bond between the Subject and the Good

For Levinas it is in the bond between the subject and the Good, the pre-originary bond with the Good, prior to freedom and non-freedom, in the creatureliness of the subject, that vulnerability is founded. This passivity is the condition by which a being shows itself to be a creature. Thus for Levinas subjectivity is described as the pre-originary bond with the Good, prior to being.

In fact, man's foreignness in the world is given a biblical reading by Levinas. The crisis of inwardness, the loss of the subject, is best expressed by the tradition and experience found within the Sacred Scriptures rather than by metaphysics or by the "end of metaphysics."(NI, 148)

Levinas asks, "Do they [the verses of the Bible] not have a right to be cited at least equal to Hölderlin and Träkl?"(NI,148) The difference between the ego and the world continues with the obligation to one's neighbor, to the other. As strangers men seek one another.(NI,149) "No one can remain in himself: the humanity of man, subjectivity, is a responsibility for the others, an extreme vulnerability." (NI, 149)

Transcendence

"We must ask if beyond the intelligibility and rationalism of identity, consciousness, the present, and being—beyond the intelligibility of immanence—the signifyingness, rationality, and rationalism of transcendence are not understood."[8]

Levinas is trying to overcome the opposition between the God of Abraham, Isaac, and Jacob, and the god of the philosophers.(GP, 155)

Levinas takes philosophy to be immanence itself. He thinks that religious thought about religious experience is no better off, that it, too, is "immanent." Levinas asks: Is it only in a discourse that does not name him that God signifies?(GP, 158-59)

Levinas reflects on the idea of God. "The idea of God is God in me, but God already breaking up the consciousness which aims at ideas . . . ."(GP, 160) The idea of the Infinite is a passivity of consciousness, or better, a passivity that is not a receptivity and so not still consciousness. It is a passivity more passive than any passivity. It is prior to all presence and is an-archical, accessible in its trace.(GP, 160-61)

> The *in* of the Infinite designates the depth of the affecting by which subjectivity is affected through this "putting" of the Infinite into it. . . . This putting in without a corresponding recollecting devastates its site like a devouring fire, catastrophizing its site. . . . It is a dazzling, where the eye takes more than it can hold, an igniting of the skin which touches and does not touch what is beyond the graspable, and burns. It is a passivity or a passion in which desire can be recognized, and in which the *"more* in the *less"* awakens by its most ardent, noblest and most ancient flame a thought given over to thinking more than it thinks.(GP, 163)

Levinas writes of "the negativity of the *in* of the Infinite" and says that it "hollows out a desire which cannot be filled, nourishes itself with its very augmentation, and is exalted as a desire, withdraws from its satisfaction in the measure that it approaches the desirable. . . ." Levinas writes, "This endless desire for what is beyond being is disinter*estedness*, transcendence—desire for the Good."(GP, 163)

Levinas maintains that for transcendence not to pass into immanence—for the love of the Infinite itself not to turn into inter*estedness*, into the erotic, back to immanence—the desirable (God) must remain separated in the desire, near but different, holy.(GP, 164)

This love of the Infinite can be only if the desirable orders me to the undesirable—the other. This is my awakening, my responsibility for my neighbor, even to substituting for him. Such responsibility is the "undoing of the nucleus of the transcendental subject."(GP, 164) The subject is broken up in the bond between the subject and the Good. The subject breaks out of himself and goes out to the other. Transcendence is self-less.

God is Infinite and desire for him cannot be satisfied, except *in* the *finite*, in the subject, who *is* only in the bond with the Good, and who breaks up and out just *as* vulnerable to the other.

Levinas writes:

> The Infinite orders me to the neighbor as a face, without being exposed to me, and does so the more imperiously that proximity narrows. The order has not been the cause of my response, nor even a question that would have preceded it in a dialogue. I find the order in my response itself, which, as a sign given to the neighbor, as a "here I am," brings me out of invisibility, out of the shadow in which my responsibility could have been evaded.[9]

Albert Camus's *The Plague* presents a protagonist who is the epitome of existentialist detachment/involvement—Dr. Bernard Rieux. In the midst of pestilence and horrible death, far from dramatizing himself, Rieux goes about his medical rounds in the most dutiful and routine way. He is a philosopher-doctor who puts his faith in man.[10]

Camus sets his novel in Oran, in 1946. He tells us that Oran is "merely a large French port on the Algerian coast." It is an ugly town—"a town without pigeons, without any trees or gardens, where you never hear the beat of wings or the rustle of leaves. . . ."(TP, 3) The chief interest of the citizens of Oran is commerce; their aim is to make money.

Oran is a microcosm of contemporary life.

> Certainly nothing is commoner nowadays than to see people working from morn till night and then proceeding to fritter away at card-tables, in cafes and in small-talk what time is left for living.(TP, 4)

In its modernity, Oran is a town in which ". . . as elsewhere, for lack of time and thinking, people have to love one another without knowing much about it."(TP, 4-5)

The town is not to be left to its banality, however. Something happens.

> When leaving his surgery on the morning of April 16, Dr. Bernard Rieux felt something soft under his foot. It was a dead rat lying in the middle of the landing.(TP, 7)

Soon Oran is infested with rats. The Ransdoc Information Bureau announces that 6,231 rats have been collected and burned in one day, April 25. On April 28, the Ransdoc Bureau announces that 8,000 rats have been collected. The epidemic and panic that follow reveal the characters. (TP, 15-16)

Camus's metaphor, plague, is tyranny of any kind. It has been taken to be the tyranny of Nazism and various totalitarianisms Camus had experienced. It is also a literal plague or pestilence. The narrator evokes images of Athens, Chinese towns, the convicts at Marseilles, the Great Wall in Provence, the Constantinople lazar-house, the Black Death, cemeteries of Milan and the streets of London.(TP, 37)

The Plague is divided into five parts, like a drama, but there are no dramatic ups and downs in the novel. The work is level, plain, monotonous. Meaning is delivered as the day-to-day "dealing with things." The struggle is sisyphean. Man is condemned by the gods, his fate, ceaselessly to push with all his strength and move the boulder up the mountain. "His rock is his thing."

When the boulder rolls back down the mountain, Sisyphus is there to push it up again—and again.

A look at Part III of Camus's novel is instructive. It is a short section. Like the third act of a play it would contain the climax. Here plague levels out discrimination of any kind. No one can be discriminated against. No one can be undervalued. But neither can anyone discriminate. No one is able to tell good from bad, better from best, life from death. The last part of the last line of Part III reads as follows: ". . . and evening after evening gave its truest, mournfullest expression to the blind endurance that had ousted love from all hearts."(TP, 168)

Camus's novel documents unbelief in anything out of the ordinary, even of the sickness that is overwhelming the town. The narrator says, "In this respect our townsfolk were like everybody else, wrapped up in themselves; in other words they were humanists: they disbelieved in pestilences. . . ."(TP, 35)

In contrast to this moral denseness is the moral acuity of Rieux and also of Tarrou, the character closest to Rieux—consciousness, understanding, clear-sightedness, or, as Tarrou's code of morals puts it: comprehension.(TP, 120-21)

A theme in Camus's novel is sympathy, a feeling for others that calls for a response to them. This responsibility makes one vulnerable to others. Transcendence of the subject or self is achieved through responsibility. (TP, 237) In *The Plague*, Tarrou's path for attaining peace is the path of sympathy. He says he is interested in learning how to become a saint. Rieux answers that heroism and sanctity do not appeal to him; what interests him is being a man.(TP, 230-31)

Later, after Tarrou succumbs to the plague, the narrator says, "So all a man could win in the conflict between plague and life was knowledge and memories. But Tarrou, perhaps, would have called that winning the match."(TP, 262)

At the end of the novel, the narrator, who turns out to be Dr. Bernard Rieux, refers to ". . . all who, while unable to be saints...strive their utmost to be healers."(TP, 278) Rieux had resolved to compile the chronicle—*The Plague*—" . . . to state quite simply what we learn in time of pestilence: that there are more things to admire in men than to despise."(TP, 278)

Levinas presents a different understanding of "transcendence" from Camus's understanding. The difference is that Levinas is writing as a philosopher who is a theist. Whether Camus was agnostic or atheist is not the main issue here. He did not explicitly found his belief in the transcending of the self for others on a bond with the Good.

Camus's humanism is Greek and also a critique of religion, specifically Christianity, as he witnessed its practice in his own time. Both in his writing and in his life he kept up the dialogue, but the conclusions of the believer were not consistently expressed by Camus. Levinas writes with exceptional profundity on Being and on the Good. He writes on desire and love for God, which cannot be satisfied except in a transcendence that is self-less, and for "the other."

Levinas's emphasis on "creatureliness" is biblical. The Greek philosophers did not have this belief that the world was created. The Greeks knew much about human vulnerability, as their great tragedies show. Nevertheless, not only do they attribute human suffering to human error and fate, but they are troubled by it in a way that Levinas is not. Suffering *is* suffering in Levinas; it is not glossed over. But it is founded in vulnerability, which is founded in creatureliness.

According to Levinas, man is passive to the Good. The Good is beyond Being. Man responds to the Good. Camus wants to leave it to man to do the good act, the ethical thing; he is suspicious of any talk about God.

Levinas does not rate "consciousness," "comprehension," "awareness" as high as Camus seems to rate them. With the ego comes disobedience. The subject knows only obedience to the Good. Camus equates "comprehension" with full humanity.

Both Levinas and Camus take ethics as responsibility for others. Their differences are important, however. Sympathy, helping out, spending oneself for others can deteriorate into self-aggrandizement and even cruelty, as Levinas knew from his experience with the Nazi era. But Camus also saw that. Perhaps what remained in Camus and in the culture he valued was a religious outlook, in so far as that implies respect and regard for what is other than the self. Both Levinas and Camus reject a philosophy of totality; whole and so-called perfect systems; totalitarianism in all its varieties, including its religious version.

Notes

1. Emmanuel Levinas, *Nine Talmudic Readings*, Introduction, trans. Annette Aronowicz (Bloomington and Indianapolis: Indiana University Press, 1990), x-xi.
2. Ibid., xi.
3. Emmanuel Levinas, "God and Philosophy," in *Collected Philosophical Papers*, 164. All further references to this essay will be cited in the text as GP.

In the works of Levinas the word "transcendence" does not have one, single meaning. The word can be understood from its use in a particular text. For instance, in *Totality and Infinity*, Section A, "Metaphysics and Transcendence," Levinas writes:

> Transcendence designates a relation with a reality infinitely distant from my own reality, yet without this distance destroying this relation and without this relation destroying this distance, as would happen with relations within the same; this relation does not become an implantation in the other and a confusion with him, does not affect the very identity of the same, its ipseity, does not silence the apology, does not become apostasy and ecstasy. (*Totality and Infinity*, 41-42.)

For Levinas, relation to any "other," whether the "other" is the personal Other (you) or the other, is transcendence. Without transcendence, all would be the same, a totality.

4. In *Collected Philosophical Papers*.
5. The "subject" has a long and varied history in philosophy. Put simply, "subject" denotes who feels, thinks, experiences, acts, is acted upon, etc., and yet who as a person with a soul transcends this description. In more modern times, what comprises the "subject" is of great interest to psychology, religion, and, of course, to the legal profession and to those who live in society under society's laws.

If the "subject" is no more than a mere mask called a "person," with "person" defined as the the sum of his own biology, psychology, sociology, literature, language, and history, then the "subject" as the originator or source of feelings, thoughts, experiences, actions, and passions disappears. The "subject" is eliminated, put out of commission.

6. "Humanism and An-archy," in *Collected Philosophical Papers*, 134-35. All further references to this essay will be cited in the text as HA.

7. "No Identity," in *Collected Philosophical Papers*, 145. All further references to this essay will be cited in the text as NI.

8. GP, 154-55.

9. Levinas, *Otherwise Than Being or Beyond Essence*, 50.

10. Albert Camus, *The Plague*, All further references to this novel will be cited in text as TP.

Bibliography

Suggested Readings

Camus, Albert. *The Plague*. Translated by Stuart Gilbert. New York: The Modern Library College Editions, 1948.

Levinas, Emmanuel. "God and Philosophy," in *Collected Philosophical Papers*. Translated by Alphonso Lingis. Boston: Martinus Nijhoff, 1987.

_____ . "Humanism and An-archy," in *Collected Philosophical Papers*. Translated by Alphonso Lingis. Boston: Martinus Nijhoff, 1987.

_____ . "No Identity," in *Collected Philosophical Papers*. Translated by Alphonso Lingis. Boston: Martinus Nijhoff, 1987.

Macquarrie, John. *Existentialism*. New York: Penguin Books, 1973.

*Works by Levinas***

L 'au-delà du verset. Paris, Minuit, 1982.

---

* The first part of this chapter, the part exclusively on Levinas, is a much revised version of a paper that I originally presented in a seminar on Recent Continental Philosophy conducted by Robert Bernasconi at Memphis State University in the fall of 1990. I am indebted to Professor Bernasconi's suggestions to the extent that I have omitted some theses I had maintained in the original paper. I am further indebted to him for reading and making several corrections in the above chapter.

** Bernasconi, Robert and Simon Critchley, ed., *Re-Reading Levinas*. (Bloomington and Indianapolis, Indiana University Press, 1991), ix.

Autrement qu'être ou au-delà de 1'essence. The Hague, Martinus Nijhoff, 1974.

Collected Philosophical Papers. Trans. Alphonso Lingis. The Hague, Martinus Nijhoff, 1987.

De l'existence à l'existant. Paris, Vrin, 1947.

Difficile Liberté. 2nd ed. Paris, Albin Michel, 1976.

Dieu qui vient à l'idée. Paris, Vrin, 1982.

En découvrant l'existence avec Husserl et Heidegqer. 3rd ed. Paris, Vrin, 1974.

Existence and Existents. Trans. Alphonso Lingis. The Hague, Martinus Nijhoff, 1978.

Éthique et Infini. Paris, Librairie Arthème Fayard, 1982.

Ethics and Infinity. Trans. Richard Cohen. Pittsburgh, Duquesne University Press, 1985.

Humanisme de l'autre homme. Montpellier, Fata Morgana, 1972.

"Le nom de Dieu d après quelques textes Talmudiques."*Archivio di Filosofia.* Rome, 1969, pp. 155-67.

Nine Talmudic Readings. Trans. Annette Aronowicz. Bloomington and Indianapolis, Indiana University Press, 1990.

Noms Propres. Montpellier, Fata Morgana, 1976.

Otherwise than Being or Beyond Essence. Trans. Alphonso Lingis. The Hague. Martinus Nijhoff, 1981.

Le temps et l'autre, Montpellier, Fata Morgana, 1979.

Totalite et Infini. The Hague, Martinus Nijhoff, 1961.

Totality and Infinity. Trans. Alphonso Lingis. Pittsburgh, Duquesne University Press, 1969.

Time and the Other. Trans. Richard Cohen. Pittsburgh, Duquesne University Press, 1987.

"The Trace of the Other." Trans. Alphonso Lingis. In *Deconstruction in Context,* ed. Mark Taylor. Chicago, University of Chicago Press, 1986, pp. 345-59.

"Wholly Otherwise." Trans. Simon Critchley. In *Re-Reading Levinas,* ed. Robert Bernasconi and Simon Critchley. Bloomington and Indianapolis, Indiana University Press, 1991 , pp. 3-10.

VIII

POPE JOHN PAUL II
MERCY IS DIVINE

K arol Wojtyla was born on May 18, 1920, at Wadowice in Galicia, the southern province of Poland. His paternal grand-father, Maciej, was a tailor in the village of Czaniec, near Andrychow, south of Krakow. Other ancestors are buried in the churchyard of Czaniec. His father, also called Karol, had served in the Austro-Hungarian Imperial army, and by the time of his birth was an administrative officer in the Polish army. His mother, Emilia (née Kaczorowska), was a schoolteacher whose parents came from Silesia. The couple already had one child, Edmund, who was fifteen in 1920. They had settled in Wadowice after their marriage. When young Karol was nearly nine, his mother died at the age of forty-five, giving birth to a stillborn girl. Karol became very attached to his godmother. Three years after the death of Emilia, Karol's brother, Edmund, died from scarlet fever.[1]

Wojtyla was early drawn to poetry, to acting, and to the theater—all outlets for his creativity. His literary interests were nationalistic and Catholic. But it was in philosophy that he came to feel at home. In 1938 he began his studies at the Jagiellonian University in Krakow. Yet Wojtyla's life was inter-rupted along with the lives of countless others by the summer of 1939. It was wartime Poland, and he had to go to work in order not to be deported for forced labor. In 1942, however, his studies took a different turn—he became a student of theology in the underground seminary. In 1945 Krakow was liberated and Wojtyla was able to come out of hiding.[2]

When he was twenty-six Karol Wojtyla was sent to Rome to

the Angelicum, the Dominican university. He returned to Poland in 1948 and was assigned to various parishes. In 1958 he was named auxiliary bishop of Krakow, no easy time to be a bishop, given the powerful Marxist forces, political and intellectual. Wojtyla was made a cardinal in 1967. He had been traveling regularly to Rome since Vatican Council II had started in 1962.[3]

Pope Paul VI died on the evening of August 6, 1978, feast of the Transfiguration. The cardinals elected Albino Luciani, patriarch of Venice, who took the name of Pope John Paul I. But this pope died on September 28, only thirty-three days after his election. On October 16, 1978, Karol Wojtyla was elected pope. He took the name Pope John Paul II.[4]

Perhaps mercy can best be contemplated, not understood, on Good Friday. How could the Father have let it happen? The encyclical *Dives in Misericordia (Rich in Mercy)* by Pope John Paul II begins with a reference to the Father.[5] Mercy and the Father are presented in Section I of the encyclical.

The Father

> It is "God, who is rich in mercy" whom Jesus Christ has revealed to us as Father: it is His very Son who, in Himself, has manifested Him and made him known to us.(DM, 7)

At the Last Supper Christ told Philip that He and the Father are one. If you see Jesus, you see the Father.(DM, 7) Christ concurs in what is happening to Him. He is not merely passive to His suffering. His will and the Father's are one.

God is "the Father of Mercies and the God of all comfort."(2 Cor. 1:3) We are urged to look at the countenance of this Father, to look at His mercy and comfort. To do so is not to "think about" his mercy; it is to experience it.(DM, 7-8)

We are confronted with "the Mystery of the Father and His love." The sufferings of the human heart in our day demand that we reflect on this mystery.(DM, 8) We are to become an-

128

thropocentric, yes. But if that is true, how much more must we become theocentric! The Church never separates God and man. God became man in Christ, and to be open to Christ it is necessary to refer to the Father and His love.(DM, 8-9)

How can we be open to the Father? He "dwells in inaccessible light." We cannot get to Him if He is inaccessible, can we? Yes, we can. The universe reveals Him; indirectly, imperfectly. The availability to God that is "achieved by the intellect seeking God by means of creatures through the visible world, falls short of vision of the Father." Christ has made him known. In and through Christ the invisible God becomes visible—in and through Christ's ". . . actions and His words, and finally through his death on the cross and His resurrection." (DM, 7-9)

In and through Christ, God becomes visible in His mercy, an attribute of divinity already named in the Old Testament as "mercy." Christ explains the mercy of God but above all He makes it incarnate. Christ personifies the mercy of God. (DM, 8-9)

John Paul II notes that present-day mentality, more than that of previous times, "seems opposed to a God of mercy. . . ."(DM, 9) Man's very achievement seems to leave no room for mercy. A closer look will show how that achievement fails, what a mixture of good and ill is evident in man. With the hope of a better future for man goes "a multitude of threats."(DM, 10)

But the "Father of mercies" is closest to man when he is suffering—faith is at the heart of man's turning "almost spontaneously" to the mercy of God. Christ through His Spirit works with human hearts. The appeal of the world today to the "Father of Mercies" is an "appeal addressed to the Church."(DM, 10)

This appeal is not only to an abstract meditation upon the mystery of God as "Father of Mercies." It is rather an appeal to have recourse, to go to that mercy in the name of Christ and in union with Him. Our Father, who "sees in secret" waits for us to come to Him in every need, Christ tells us. He waits for us "to study His mystery," the "mystery of the Father and His love."(DM, 11) All need mercy, even without knowing it.(DM, 11)

Christ

Again, it is especially to the poor that Christ makes the Father present.

> Before His own townspeople, in Nazareth, Christ refers to the prophet Isaiah: "The Spirit of the Lord is upon me, because he has anointed me to preach good news to the poor. He has sent me to proclaim release to the captives and recovery of sight to the blind, to set at liberty those who are oppressed, to proclaim the acceptable year of the Lord." (Luke 4: 18-19) (DM, 11)

For the first time [in Luke] Christ declares Himself Messiah and follows up this announcement by the actions and words that we read in the Gospel. Thus Christ makes the Father present among men. Section II of the encyclical shows how Christ makes the Father's mercy present.

All the miserable are to receive mercy. For sinners the Messiah is the clear sign of the love of God—in Christ's day and in our own. He came for all but "... especially the poor, those without means of subsistence, those deprived of their freedom, the blind who cannot see the beauty of creation, those living with broken hearts, or suffering from social injustice, and finally sinners."(DM, 11)

One notices that Christ does not inveigh against the drug lords, the pimps and prostitutes, the homosexually active, the mean judges of all of these. For who is more miserable than any one of these, including the one who reads the newspapers and watches television only to bewail what he learns. No. To these He preaches *good news*—release, sight, freedom—the glorious time set by the Lord.

Later, when John the Baptist sends messengers to inquire who Christ is, the same answer is given as was given when He began His teaching at Nazareth.

> Go and tell John what it is that you have seen and heard: the blind receive their sight, the lame walk, lepers are cleansed, and the deaf hear, the dead are raised up, the poor have the good news preached to them.

He ends with: "And blessed is he who takes no offense at me!" (DM, 12)

Mercy *is* love that manifests itself to the limited and the weak, physically and morally.(DM, 12) Who believes he needs mercy if he is confident of his strength, confident in his own gifts, his race, nationality, his family background, his looks, intelligence, cleverness, athletic prowess, orderliness? Name anything, from a near-infinite list, that human beings *pride themselves* in and you have something that inhibits the knowledge (and feeling) that the mercy of God *must be had.*

Yet is nothing to be done, no building put up, no book written, no streets paved, no space explored? Are we all to want to be disabled? Yes. We are to realize that we are disabled—by our sins and by the lack of all that we could have, and that all of these feats of ours are dependent on God, that as we learned as children in our catechism, if God forgot us for one second, we would not even exist but would pass into nothingness.

The truth that Christ reveals God as "rich in mercy" is not just the subject of a teaching; it is a reality made present to us by Christ.(DM,12)

> *Making the Father present as love and mercy is,* in Christ's own consciousness, the fundamental touchstone of His mission as the Messiah; this is confirmed by the words that He uttered first in the synagogue at Nazareth and later in the presence of His disciples and of John the Baptist's messengers.(DM, 12)

Mercy is one of the principal themes of Christ's preaching, first in parables. Parables "express better the essence of things": the prodigal son, the Good Samaritan, the merciless servant, the Good Shepherd, the woman who searches for her lost coin. The Gospel of Luke treats these especially, a Gospel that merits the title "the Gospel of mercy."(DM, 12)

A parable is a story that conveys meaning indirectly by the use of a comparison. How is it that such a story "expresses better the essence of things"? It does so because story is life and life is story. Life is conflict and so is story. No conflict, no story. The man helped by the Good Samaritan presented him with a problem, and the Good Samaritan solved it according to the mercy of God.

> Christ in revealing the love-mercy of God, at the same time *demanded from people* that they also should be guided in their lives by love and mercy. This requirement forms part of the very essence of the messianic message, and constitutes the heart of the Gospel *ethos*. The Teacher expresses this both through the medium of the commandment which he describes as "the greatest," and also in the form of a blessing, when in the Sermon on the mount He proclaims: "Blessed are the merciful, for they shall obtain mercy."(DM, 13)

The heart of the Gospel *ethos;* to show mercy is the heart of Christian ethics. Christian ethics is without life, *it is not,* if it is not merciful at the core; a heart of mercy is a Christian heart.

The Old Testament

In Section III of *Dives in Misericordia*, Pope John Paul II explains the meaning of the term "mercy" and the content of the concept "mercy."(DM, 13)

He begins with the concept of "mercy." The People of God in the Old Testament knew the concept of mercy. They had a special experience of the mercy of God, socially and individually. Many times they had broken the covenant with God. When the prophets and others called them to awareness, they sought mercy. Examples abound: the beginning of the history of the Judges, the prayer of Solomon at the inauguration of the Temple, part of the prophetic work of Micah, the consoling assurances given by Isaiah, the cry of Jews in exile, and the renewal of the covenant after the return from exile.(DM, 14)

> In the preaching of the prophets, *mercy* signifies *a special power of love,* which *prevails over the sin and infidelity* of the chosen people.(DM, 14)

But the sin is individual, too. It is the interior "languishing in the state of guilt or enduring every kind of suffering and misfortune."(DM, 14-15) David, Job, Esther are some examples.(DM, 15)

The basic experience of the chosen people at the Exodus is the pattern. The Lord saw the affliction of His people and chose to deliver them. Thus the prophet perceived the love and compassion of the Lord, and the people as a whole and each individual grounded their confidence on the mercy of God, "which can be invoked whenever tragedy strikes."(DM,15)

The God of mercies loves with the love of a spouse, who pardons sins and even infidelity and betrayal.(DM,14)

> All the subtleties of love become manifest in the Lord's mercy towards those who are His own: He is their Father, for Israel is His firstborn son; the Lord is also the bridegroom of her whose new name the prophet proclaims: *Ruhamah*, "Beloved" or "she has obtained pity."(DM, 15)

Pope John Paul's encyclical translates as if the Lord can be "exasperated" by infidelity and yet instead of calling off the relationship, "His tenderness and generous love for those who are His own . . . overcomes his anger."(DM, 15-16) Not only is God Himself merciful, each son and daughter of Israel is merciful toward one another.

MERCY IS THE CONTENT OF INTIMACY WITH THEIR LORD. (DM, 16)

Thus concludes the encyclical's treatment of the concept of "mercy." The rest of Section III treats of the use in the Old Testament of terms naming concepts having contents different from but related to that of "mercy." The people in misfortune and especially in sin are encouraged to appeal for mercy. They are reminded of God's mercy when they fail or lose trust in Him. They give thanks and glory to God for His mercy whenever it is made evident in the life of the group or in the life of the individual.(DM,16)

In some sense God's mercy is contrasted with His justice and often is shown as more powerful and more profound than justice. Justice is indeed a virtue in man, and "in God signifies

transcendent perfection," but love is more "primary and fundamental" than justice, and thus "greater."(DM, 16)

> Love, so to speak, conditions justice and, in the final
> analysis, justice serves love. The primacy and superior-
> ity of love vis-a-vis justice—this is a mark of the whole
> of revelation—are *revealed precisely through mercy.*(DM,
> 16-17)

The psalmists and prophets used the term "justice" to mean
salvation by God and His mercy.(DM, 17) God hates nothing
He has made. His justice and mercy are different one from the
other, but they are not in opposition. The mystery of creation is
ultimately the root of the relationship between God's justice
and mercy.(DM, 17)

The *mystery of election* refers to all of the human family. Both
the Old Testament and the New tell of it. As the revelation
ends, on the night before Christ dies, He says to Philip: "Have
I been with you so long, and yet you do not know me...? He
who has seen me has seen the Father."(DM, 17)

The Prodigal Son

The parable of the prodigal son as presented in the fourth
section of the encyclical expresses the essence of divine mercy
in an especially clear way, even though the word "mercy" is not
used. The mystery of mercy is shown as the drama of the
father's love and the son's sin is acted out. The prodigal son is
the pattern for every breach between God and those who are
supposed to be in a covenanted love with him, beginning with
Adam and extending to all individuals who have sinned—all
men and women—and to groups of people, too.(DM, 18-19)

The prodigal son wastes his inheritance on riotous living, is
cast out by his fellow sinners, wishes he were back with his
father, even if that means inhabiting his father's pigpen. He
returns, his father sees him on the way home, and runs out to
hug him to himself—overjoyed that he is back—no matter in
what condition.

The analogy between the son's condition and that of every

man and woman is between the interior state of the prodigal son and that of every man and woman. What *seems* to to be the focus of loss is material goods; what *is* the focus of loss is the dignity the son has as a member of the household of the father.(DM, 18-19)

The son sees that he ought now to be glad to be even an employee in his father's house, as humiliating as that would be. He has become willing to lower his status, and this has happened because of his suffering.(DM, 19-20)

Pope John Paul II writes:

> In the parable of the prodigal son, the term "justice" is not used even once; just as in the original text the term "mercy" is not used either. *Nevertheless, the relationship between justice and love, that is manifested as mercy*, is inscribed with great exactness in the content of the Gospel parable. It becomes more evident that love is transformed into mercy when it is necessary to go beyond the precise norm of justice—precise and often too narrow.(DM, 20)

The father of the prodigal son is faithful to his fatherhood, to himself. This faithfulness is marked by his compassion, an emotion that derives from the deep affection he bears his son. On a deeper level, the cause of the emotion is the saving of the fundamental good of his son's humanity, his human dignity. This dignity is saved because it is "found again."(DM, 21) The joyous emotion can be explained as follows: "The father's fidelity to himself is totally concentrated upon the humanity of the lost son, upon his dignity."(DM, 21)

The love that springs from the very essence of fatherhood has the interior form of the love that is called *agape*. This love can reach to every human misery, especially to moral misery—sin. The person who is the object of this mercy does not feel humiliated but restored.(DM, 22)

Pope John Paul II calls attention to the fact that we have prejudices about mercy. Such prejudices come from viewing mercy from the inside, seeing mercy as a relationship of inequality, one that belittles the receiver. But the prodigal son, experiencing mercy, sees himself truly. Seeing the truth is a form of humility. He then becomes a particular good for his father, a good that the father sees as a mystery of truth and love. The father seems to forget all the evil that the son has committed.(DM, 22)

The son is converted; love is expressed and mercy is seen as present in the human world. Mercy is more than compassion; it is a restoration to value that "draws good from all the forms of evil" in the world and in man.(DM, 22-23) ". . . mercy constitutes the fundamental content of the messianic message of Christ and the constitutive power of His mission."(DM, 23) Mercy refuses to be conquered by evil. It overcomes evil with good.(DM, 23)

Mother of Mercy

Mary obtained mercy as no other person has. She also made possible by the sacrifice of her heart her own sharing in revealing God's mercy. Her sacrifice is intimately linked with that of her Son; she stood at the foot of the Cross. (DM, 30)

> *No one has experienced to the same degree as the Mother of the crucified One,* the mystery of the cross, the overwhelming encounter of divine transcendent justice with love: that "kiss" given by mercy to justice.(DM, 30)

She is the Mother of Mercy—our Lady of mercy, Mother of divine mercy.(DM, 30) In contact with moral and physical evil, this merciful love is manifested. Her mercy is based upon "the unique tact of her maternal heart."(DM, 31) By her intercession she obtains for us the graces of eternal salvation. She takes care of us.(DM, 31-32)

Shusaku Endo's short story "Mothers" is the tale of a son visiting the island of his dead mother.[6] He is met by a man sent by the church to greet him. The visitor asks how the priest, "the Father," is. He receives no answer. He had met the priest of the island in Tokyo, and had asked him if he knew Father Fukabori, a priest whom the visitor/narrator, a writer, had met a year earlier when he had been visiting a fishing village an hour from

Nagasaki. Father Fukabori had taught him how to deep-sea fish and had also helped him with his research. The narrator says that the purpose of his trip had been to visit the *kakure*, descendants of some of the original Christian converts in the seventeenth century who had over the years corrupted the religious practices.(M, 161-71)

The *kakure*, to whose homes Father Fukabori had taken him, had refused to be reconverted to Catholicism. They had been isolated and their version of Christianity was a mix of Shinto, Buddhism, and local superstition. The *kakure* were scattered throughout the Goto and Ikitsuki Islands.

The narrator had tried to get more information from the country priest but the latter had resisted him. Nevertheless, a month later he had received from this second priest an invitation to visit, saying that some of the *kakure* who lived in his parish would be willing to show their religious icons and copies of their prayers.(M, 171)

Now on this trip the narrator asks again for the *kakure* and is told that they live in the mountains. In spite of the physical weakness he suffers from the chest surgery he has undergone seven years previously, he decides to make the long and arduous trip to the *kakure* "secluded mountain fastnesses or inaccessible coastlines."(M,172)

"Mothers" is a story of betrayal and the hope for mercy, a hope that is almost indistinguishable from despair. The narrative moves back and forth between the narrator/writer's memory of his mother and his search for the *kakure* and for more information about them. He had forsaken his mother after he had abandoned any hope of religious faith for himself, and the *kakure* were apostates. His own self-preservation and fleshly weakness are multiplied and magnified in the *kakure*. It is as if in gaining knowledge of them, he can understand and perhaps absolve himself. But his own efforts cannot accomplish what he wants them to accomplish. Nor can the *kakure* help themselves. His sole salvation—and theirs—is in the plea for mercy.

> We beseech thee, as we weep and moan in this vale of tears. . . . Intercede for us, and turn eyes filled with mercy upon us.(M, 194)

As the narrator searches out the *kakure*, he dreams of his mother.

> I dreamed of my mother. In my dream I had just been brought out of the operating theatre, and was sprawled out on my bed like a corpse. A rubber tube connected to an oxygen tank was thrust into my nostril, and intravenous needles pierced my right arm and leg, carrying blood from the transfusion bottles dangling over my head.(M, 172)

His mother is holding his hand in the dream, and yet he has no remembrance of his ever having been ill with his mother holding his hand. He says, "Normally the image of my mother that pops into my mind is the figure of a woman who lived her life fervently."(M, 173)

He can remember when his father and mother were still together and he was five years old. His mother is practicing the violin. She practices the same melody over and over again.(M, 173)

His father leaves her and she adopts a solitary life.

> Just as she had once played her violin in search of the one true note, she subsequently adopted a stern, solitary life in quest of the one true religion. On wintry mornings, at the frozen fissure of dawn, I often noticed a light in her room. I knew what she was doing in there. She was fingering the beads of her rosary and praying. Eventually she would take me with her on the first Hankyu-line train of the day and set out for Mass. On the deserted train I slouched back in my seat and pretended to be rowing a boat. But occasionally I would open my eyes and see my mother's fingers gliding along those rosary beads.(M, 174)

Now the narrator shifts his attention to the history of Christianity on the island village. The persecution of the Christians began in 1607 and was at its worst between 1615 and 1617. The narrator studies the awful accounts of the martyrdoms. The loss in the count of Christians between the seventeenth century and the present was about one-third. And, of course, there were the *kakure*, who evidently were becoming fewer in number as the older ones died out and the younger ones abandoned the old practices.(M, 175-79)

The narrator remembers that he learned to lie to his mother. He says he must have had a complex in his mother's regard; her religious zeal stifled him. The more she pressed religious prac-tice on him, the more he learned to live without her approval. He finally stopped going to Mass altogether.(M, 179-80)

But he has made the journey to his mother's grave in the Catholic cemetery in Fuchu countless times—the day he gradu-ated from the university, the day before he boarded ship for France for further studies, again when he fell ill and had to return to Japan, the day he was married, the day he went into the hospital.(M, 184-85)

> Mother's grave is small. My heart constricts whenever I look at that tiny grave marker. I pluck the wild grasses that surround it. With buzzing wings, insects swarm around me as I work in solitude. There is no other sound.(M, 185)

His mother died without him. He had been at the house of someone his mother could never have approved and doing something that would have caused her to weep—looking at obscene pictures. He had been at Tamura's, where his mother had forbidden him to go when she found out that his father ran a whorehouse.(M,185)

Now in his search for information on the *kakure*, he admits to himself the source of his interest.

> But I am interested in the *kakure* for only one reason— because they are the offspring of apostates. Like their ancestors, they cannot utterly abandon their faith; in-stead they live out their lives, consumed by remorse and dark guilt and shame.(M,186)

The *kakure* behave like a secret society. They have pretended to be Buddhists. Scourges they had made to use in order to assuage the guilt of their religious betrayal can be found. Their prayers reflect their humiliation.(M, 188-89)

> Santa Maria, Mother of God, be merciful to us sinners in the hour of death. We beseech thee, as we weep and moan in this vale of tears. Intercede for us, and turn eyes filled with mercy upon us. (M, 189)

The narrator continues to dream of his mother and in situations that are not a literal reflection of anything he can remember. What he does come to realize is that he has imposed upon his mother the figure of the Mater Dolorosa, the Holy Mother of Sorrows, an image his mother used to own. (M, 191) The *kakure*, too, had let go of the teachings on God the Father and had replaced these "by a yearning after a Mother. . . ."(M, 196)

> In this vale of tears, intercede for us; and turn eyes filled with mercy upon us. I hummed the melody of the prayer that I had just learned. . . . I muttered the supplication that the *kakure* continually intoned.(M, 196)

Reflection on the encyclical *Rich in Mercy* by Pope John Paul II and on "Mothers" by Endo places each of us within the need for the mercy of God, however that is extended to us. It also reminds, perhaps, warns, us to show mercy to others. If we want a justice that is fairness, and if that means we want what we deserve, we may not end up too well off. We had better want and grant mercy, trying not to forget the "board" in our own eye as we mistakenly contemplate the need to remove the "speck" from our brother's eye. "Blessed are the merciful; mercy shall be theirs."

Notes

1. Peter Hebblethwaite and Ludwig Kaufmann, *John Paul II: A Pictorial Biography* (New York: McGraw-Hill Book Co., 1979), 14-16, *passim.*
2. Ibid., 24-44, *passim.*
3. Ibid., 46-64, *passim.*
4. Ibid., 72.
5. Pope John Paul II, *Dives in Misericordia [On the Mercy of God]* (Boston: Daughters of St. Paul, 1980), 5. All further references to this encyclical will be cited in the text as DM.
6. Shusaku Endo, "Mothers," in *Substance of Things Hoped For,* selected with an Introduction by John B. Breslin, S.J. (New York: Doubleday, 1988), 168-96. All further references to this story will be cited in the text as M.

Works by John Paul II are in various genres—drama, poetry, philosophy, theology (systematic, pastoral, spiritual, etc.)—and so numerous that no attempt has been made here to list them. A complete bibliography of primary sources, and also of secondary sources, is subject for a full-length book or a dissertation.

Part Two

IX

ST. THOMAS AQUINAS
JUSTICE AND HAPPINESS

In Part II-II of St.Thomas's *Summa Theologica,* in the "Treatise on Prudence and Justice," Question 58 is entitled "On Justice." This Question is divided into twelve articles, with each article itself set forth as a question. The twelve articles are as follows:

Article 1: Whether justice is fittingly defined as being the perpetual and constant will to render to each one his right?

Article 2: Whether justice is always toward another?

Article 3: Whether justice is a virtue?

Article 4: Whether justice is in the will as its subject?

Article 5: Whether justice is a general virtue?

Article 6: Whether justice, as a general virtue, is essentially the same as all virtue?

Article 7: Whether there is a particular besides a general justice?

Article 8: Whether particular justice has a special matter?

Article 9: Whether justice is about the passions?

Article 10:Whether the mean of justice is the real mean?

Article 11:Whether the act of justice is to render to each one his own?

Article 12:Whether justice stands foremost among all moral virtues?

As always in St. Thomas, a simple "yes" or "no" is not satisfactory. He is interested in making distinctions as he answers the questions. But we can begin with the "yes" and "no" and then proceed to the details of an argument. Here are the "yes" and "no" answers to the twelve questions posed on justice: (1)yes; (2)yes; (3)yes; (4)yes; (5)yes; (6)no; (7)yes; (8)yes; (9)no; (10)yes; (11)yes; (12)yes.

We can pick out three of the above and treat them in at least as much detail as space permits by studying the essential part of each article, the "I answer that." These three are Articles 1, 2, and 9.

Article 1: St.Thomas says that this definition of justice is correct if it is understood properly. Every virtue is a habit that is the principle (starting point) of a good act. Thus each virtue must be defined by means of the good act bearing on the matter proper to that virtue. The proper matter of the virtue of justice consists of those things that belong to our intercourse with other men. Furthermore, for an act to be virtuous, it must be voluntary, stable, and firm. Aristotle says in *Ethics* ii, 4, that for an act to be virtuous, first, it must be done knowingly; second, it must be done by choice and for a due end; third, it must be done immovably. The first is included in the second, since what is done through ignorance is done involuntarily (*Ethics*, iii, 1). Thus the definition of justice mentions the will first, and then constancy and perpetuity. St. Thomas offers his own definition of justice and then Aristotle's, saying that they are the same. St.Thomas: Justice is a habit whereby a man renders to each one his due by a constant and perpetual will. Aristotle: Justice is a habit whereby a man is said to be capable of doing just actions in accordance with his choice. (*Ethics* v, 5)

Article 2: According to St.Thomas, justice is always toward another. He refers to Question 57, Article 1, where he has said that justice by its name implies equality. It thus denotes essentially relation to another, since a thing is equal, not to itself, but to another. He then refers again to Question 57, Article 1, and to I-II, Question 113, Article 1, where he has said that it belongs to justice to rectify human acts. Thus the otherness demanded by justice has to be between two beings capable of action. Actions belong to subjects or persons, to wholes, not to parts, forms, or powers. We do not say the hand strikes but rather that the man strikes with his hand, etc., even though such expressions (as "the hand strikes," "the heat makes a thing hot," etc.) may be used metaphorically. Justice, then, demands a distinction of persons, and consequently is only in one man towards another. Metaphorically, we may speak of the various principles of action in one and the same man—the reasonable, the irascible [spirited, as in the emotion of anger] or concupiscible [desirous, as in sexual attraction]—as if they were each agents, or actors. Metaphorically, we say that in one and the same man there is justice insofar as reason commands the irascible and the concupiscible and these two obey reason. Aristotle calls this "metaphorical justice." (*Ethics*, v, 11)

Article 9: The answer to this question is found, first, from the subject of justice, that is, from the will, whose movements or acts are not passions, as Thomas has shown in III, Question 22, Article 3, and in Question 59, Article 4. It is only the sensitive appetite whose movements are called passions. Temperance, which is in the concupiscible part of the soul, and fortitude, which is in the irascible part of the soul, are about the passions. Justice is not. The answer to the question is found, second, on the part of the matter. The matter is what something is about, and justice is about a man's relations with another. But we are not directed immediately to another by the internal passions. Therefore, justice is not about the passions.

For St.Thomas, then, following Aristotle, justice has to do with our relations with those outside ourselves, individuals and groups outside ourselves. Moreover, it has to do with the will, what St.Thomas calls the rational appetite. The will is directed by the intellect. Thus justice will have a close connection with truth, the correspondence between thought and reality.

Happiness

In Part I-II of St. Thomas's *Summa Theologica*, Question 2 is entitled "Of Those Things in Which Man's Happiness Consists." He answers in eight articles. The answers and reasons are quite unassailable, and they are multiple. We can limit ourselves to the very direct ones that appear in the sections called "On the contrary." Then, a sentence or two will assess how contemporary man seems to view the matter.

Article 1: Does man's happiness consist in wealth? No, and essentially because, as Boethius says in *Consolation of Philosophy* ii, "wealth shines in giving rather than in hoarding: for the miser is hateful, whereas the generous man is applauded." This position is only tenable because Aquinas has first made the claim that man's good consists in retaining happiness rather than in spreading it (Q.2, Art. 1, On the contrary), an interesting insight in light of contemporary talk about "spreading sunshine and happiness." Here as elsewhere the classical thinkers show little presumption.

Article 2: Does man's happiness consist in honors? No, and here Aquinas has recourse to Aristotle's *Ethics*, i, 5. Happiness is in the happy. Honor, however, is not in the honored but in the one who does the honoring.(Q.2, Art. 2, On the contrary) The puffed up vanity of our times may disagree, feeling that honor is enjoyed by the one honored and so is *in* him.

Article 3: Does man's happiness consist in fame or glory? No. Happiness is man's true good, and fame and glory are false. Again, Aquinas quotes Boethius's *Consolation of Philosophy* iii: "... many owe their renown to the lying reports spread among the people. Can anything be more shameful? For those who receive false fame, must needs blush at their own praise."(Q.2, Art. 3, On the contrary) But we may well fear from what we gather from the media that fame is exulted in perhaps more when it is not gotten honestly. Some may actually enjoy the fact that they have duped others, and call this enjoyment happiness.

Article 4: Does man's happiness consist in power? No, again. Happiness is the perfect good. Power is most imperfect. Boethius, *Consolation of Philosophy* iii: "... the power of man cannot relieve the gnawings of care, nor can it avoid the thorny path of anxiety." And also from Boethius: "Think you a man is powerful who is surrounded by attendants, whom he inspires with fear indeed, but whom he fears still more?" (Q.2, Art. 4, On the contrary) Yet the "show" of power may be so coveted that it passes for happiness.

Article 5: Does man's happiness consist in any bodily good? No, because while man surpasses all other animals in happiness, many of them surpass him in bodily goods. The elephant has greater longevity; the lion has greater strength; the stag is more fleet.(Q. 2, Art. 5, On the contrary) The emphasis today on bodily beauty and on fitness would perhaps contend that from sheer aesthetics and/or a sense of "feeling good" bodily good is happiness.

Article 6: Does man's happiness consist in pleasure? Boethius once more supplies the answer in *Consolation of Philosophy* iii: "Any one that chooses to look back on his past excesses, will perceive that pleasures have a sad ending: and if they can render a man happy, there is no reason why we should not say that the very beasts are happy too."(Q.2, Art. 6, On the contrary) Many, however, would argue that not to have experienced certain pleasures, even in excess, is "not to have lived."

Article 7: Does some good of the soul constitute man's happiness? No, and Aquinas's authority is St. Augustine's *On Christian Doctrine,* i, 22. ". . . that which constitutes the life of happiness is to be loved for its own sake." Aquinas then says that man is not to be loved for his own sake. Whatever is in man is to be loved for the sake of God. Thus happiness cannot consist in any good of man's soul.(Q.2, Art. 7, On the contrary) This answer, even when we think we are religious, may surprise us, so centered are we in our own day on man and on self. We tend to think it praiseworthy to spend all of our time thinking of our souls or psyches, or the souls and psyches of others. Here we have two saints, both brilliant minds, tell us that this view is mistaken.

Article 8: Does any created good constitute man's happiness?

Of course not. Augustine in the *City of God*, xix, 26: "As the soul is the life of the body, so God is man's life of happiness: of Whom it is written: 'Happy is that people whose God is the Lord.'"(Psalm 143:15) (Q.2, Art. 8, On the contrary) Think of the efforts, counsels, money, time spent on trying to be happy! And here it is in Him in Whom we live and move and have our being!

X

St. Thomas Aquinas and Karol Wojtyla
Intention, Person, Communion, Transcendence, and Mercy

In St. Thomas, "intention" may be defined as follows:
1. as opposed to "execution," used of activity, cognitive and appetitive, which as such produces no physical change; 2. as opposed to "volition," the reaching to an end rather than the attainment of an objective; 3. as opposed to "election," the willing of an end, not of what is subordinate to an end. Both volition and election are intentional in sense no. 1[1]

Question 12, I-II, of the *Summa Theologica*, is entitled "Of Intention."[2] Question 12 is found in the "Treatise on the Last End," which is happiness (Q. 1, Art. 7, On the contrary), namely, the vision of the Divine Essence (Q. 3, Art. 8, I answer that). In Questions 6-21 St. Thomas treats of human (moral) acts. The focus is on the human will and its willing. Questions 18 and 19 are especially useful for an understanding of Question 12. For St. Thomas intention is not comprehensive of goodness.

Intention is an act of the will. (Q. 12, On the contrary) The argument goes as follows:

—Intention signifies *to tend to something.*

—Both the action of the mover and the movement of the thing moved tend to something.

—That the movement of the thing moved tends to anything is due to the action of the mover.

—Therefore, intention belongs first and principally to that which moves to the end (we say that an architect

or anyone who is in authority by his command moves
others to that which he intends).
—The will moves all the other powers of the soul to the
end. (Q. 9, Art.1)
—It is evident, then, that intention, properly speaking, is
an act of the will. (Q. 12, Art. 1, I answer that)

St. Thomas says that intention is an act of the will in regard
to the end. The will stands in a threefold relation to the end. 1)
The will is related to the end "absolutely" in what is called
"volition." We will absolutely, without qualification, to be
healthy, for example. 2) The will is related to the end as its place
of rest in what is called enjoyment. 3) The will is related to the
end as the term towards which something is ordained in what
is called "intention." What we intend we will have, but we will
have it by means of something else. (Q. 12, Art. 1, Reply Obj. 4)

To examine the role of intention in human or moral acts, we
have to note what St. Thomas says about the goodness of an
action. Question 18 is entitled "Of the Good and Evil of Human
Acts, in General." St. Thomas says that the good or evil of an
action depends on its fullness of being or its lack of that fullness. Not only actions but indeed all things are as good or as
evil as they enjoy fullness of being or its lack. (Q. 18, Art. 1, I
answer that, in which there is also a reference to *Summa
Theologica*, I, Q. 5, Arts. 1 & 3, where St. Thomas discusses the
relation between goodness and being)

Actions, as well as things, are good or are lacking in goodness according as they are of a certain kind or genus. They are
as good as they have the fullness of being proper to a given
genus, the genus being that part of a thing or action which
belongs also to others differing from it in species.

The species is a subdivision of the genus. Each thing has
fullness of being from what gives it its species. A natural thing
has its primary goodness from its form, which gives it its species. A moral action has its primary goodness from its suitable
object. For this reason, the action is called good in its genus. An
example is given: making use of what is one's own. The primary evil in moral actions is also from the object, and again an

example is given: taking what belongs to another. This action is said to be evil in its genus, "genus here standing for species, just as we apply the term mankind to the whole human species." (Q. 18, Art. 2, I answer that)

What is this *object*? The *object* is not the matter *which* (a thing is made), but the matter *about which* (something is done). The *object* is the form of the act; it gives the act its species. (Q. 18, Art. 2, Reply Obj. 2)

In Question 12 St. Thomas offers a "measure" of the goodness of an action.

> ... the ... proportion of an action to its effect is the measure of its goodness. (Q. 12, Art. 2, Reply Obj. 3)

The goodness of the action is not caused by the goodness of the effect, yet an action is good from the fact that it can produce a good effect. (Q. 12, Art. 2, Reply Obj. 3)

The effect we intend is good health; the means we intend are actions which are as good as they are proportionate to the effect. If someone were to decide for a total fast of two weeks as a means to good health, the goodness of the action would have to be measured by the proportion of the action of the fast to its effect. Similarly, if someone were to decide for two weeks at a health resort as a means to good health, the goodness of the action would have to be measured by the proportion of the action of taking the holiday to its effect. In the case of the fast, the effect might be poorer health, and in the case of the trip, the effect might be financial impoverishment out of proportion to the improvement in health effected by the two weeks at the health resort.

Thus for St. Thomas even when we consider intention as opposed to execution, that is, when we understand the action to be only cognitive or appetitive, or only reaching to the end rather than attaining an objective, or willing an end and not what is subordinate to an end, the goodness or evil of the action itself, considered as a kind of action, is determining, and the determinant is the proportion of the action to its effect. It is thus easy to see that circumstances alter the goodness or evil of such an action since circumstances would enter into the measurement of the proportion. (Cf. Q. 18, Art. 3)

St. Thomas says that a human action has a "fourfold goodness": 1) that which, as an action, it derives from its genus; as much as the action has of being so much does it have of goodness; 2) according to its species, which is derived from its suitable object; 3) from its circumstances, in respect, as it were, of its accidents; 4) from its end, to which it is compared as to the cause of its goodness. (Q. 18, Art. 4, I answer that) Moreover, if any one of the four is missing, that is, if there is a single defect, the action is not "good simply." It has to be good in all four ways. (Q. 18, Art. 4, Reply Obj. 3)

Question 19 is entitled "Of the Goodness and Malice of the Interior Act of the Will." It is in the analysis of the interior act of the will that St. Thomas brings together intention and action. The goodness of the will resides in the fact that a man wills that which is good. Goodness is not from the end but from the object. But the end is the object of the will, although not of the other human powers. With regard to an act of the will, the goodness derived from the object does not differ from the goodness derived from the end. (Q. 19, Art. 2, Reply Obj. 1)

In the acts of powers other than the will, these two—what is taken from the object and what is taken from the end—differ. With regard to an act of the will, the goodness from the object and that from the end may differ accidentally, for example, one end can depend on another end, one act of the will on another act. (Q. 19, Art. 2, Reply Obj. 1; Reply Obj. 2)

"Intention" is an act of the will (Q. 12, Art. 1, I answer that), the tending toward something. "Intention" belongs to that which moves to the "end." The "end" is the desirable for its own sake. Human "action" is that which has its goodness dependent on something else, namely, on four sources—genus, species, circumstances, end. The "object" is "that which" is done, the concrete thing. St. Thomas says that with regard to an act of the will, the goodness derived from the object does not differ from the goodness derived from the end.

To help someone in need is an "end," something desirable for its own sake; to give bread to the hungry (real bread to a real man who is hungry) is an "object," a concrete thing to do. The goodness of helping someone in need (an end) is the same as the goodness of giving bread to the hungry (an object). If intention is the reaching to an end and the willing of an end, which, as such produces no physical change, and if action is what has its goodness dependent on genus, species, circumstances, and end, then with regard to the will, intention and action are brought together. Goodness is from the object; with regard to the will, the object and the end coincide. Thus intention, being what tends toward the end, is included. The goodness of the will does depend on the intention of the end. (Q. 19, Art. 7, On the contrary)

Nevertheless, the degree of goodness in the will does not depend on the degree of goodness in the intention. The intention can be good while the will is evil, and the intention can be better and the will less good. (Q. 19, Art. 8, On the contrary) An object ordained to the intended end may not be proportionate to that end. To give less than what it costs to build a house while intending to cover such costs is not to realize one's intention. To be unable to cover the cost because of a theft one has suffered between the intention and the action keeps one from realizing one's intentions. (Q. 19, Art. 8)

In St. Thomas each object, material and immaterial, has its own good. Moral or human good is fourfold, the end being part of what makes an act good. Since intention, necessary for goodness but not sufficient in itself, is what tends toward an end, this, too, is a part of goodness. The measure of the goodness of an action is the proportion of the action to its effect. Thus intention is not comprehensive of goodness. Goodness is rather the ratio between the action and its effect. This ratio is computed with the following variables: kind of action (good or bad in itself, depending on its fullness of being or lack of such fullness), specific action (appropriate to its object), circumstances, and end (including intention and its realization).

In the chapter entitled "The Personal Structure of Self-Determination," Chapter 3, found in Part Two ("The Transcendence of the Person in Action") of *The Acting Person* by Karol Wojtyla

(Pope John Paul II), "intention" is distinguished from "intent."[3]

Wojtyla has in the background of his treatment of "intention" the history of the use of the term. He writes: "An intentional act of man's experience consists in being oriented or directed outward toward an object."(TAP, 126) He notes that this "going out toward an object" takes place in acts of volition and in acts of cognition. He calls the act of the will an "intent" and an act of cognition an "intention."(TAP, 126)

Wojtyla sets his discussion in the context of an analysis of the will. He states explicitly that his procedure differs from the traditional approach. What does he mean? Earlier philosophers analyzed the will and its intentionality. Wojtyla's claim is that his own analysis is directed to a study of "the roots of the will," which grow out from "the structure of the person."(TAP, 124-25)

The phrase that troubles Wojtyla is "rational appetite," the traditional definition of "will." He admits that there was good reason for this view of the will; the will does typically have an "urge toward good as its object and end."(TAP, 124) This urge toward the good as object and end brought about the emphasis on intentionality. Wojtyla maintains that the intentionality of the will does not completely account for all of the activity of the will, nor does restricting oneself to looking at the will in its intentionality give insight into "the dynamism and potentiality appropriate to it [the will]."(TAP,124-25)

The use of the word "appetite" with the word "rational" is a difficulty for Wojtyla. Appetite suggests striving but it also suggests desire. Desire points "only in the direction of what is *happening* in man, to what lies beyond the range of his conscious decision."(TAP, 125) From one perspective the phrase "rational appetite" contains two words that are in contradiction to one another; from another perspective, the more conative, the word "appetite" becomes neutralized and the contradiction is removed.(TAP, 125)

Viewed semantically the word "appetite" cannot be attributed to the will—at least not if the word connotes "sensual passivity and as such originates and unfolds on its own, spontaneously, outside of conscious choice and decision."(TAP, 125)

Wojtyla maintains that interest in the semantics of the issue is crucial, since he is trying "to find a definition that would be in all respects adequate for every human willing."(TAP, 125)

It is because Wojtyla wants to underline the difference between the intentionality of cognition and that of volition that he calls the first an "intention" and the second an "intent."(TAP, 125-26) ". . . 'to know' or 'to understand' and 'to will' are dissimilar."(TAP, 126) Again, the first is "tending toward something" and the second is "being intent on something."(TAP,126) The two have very different consequences for both the subject and the object.(TAP, 126)

> In this study we view thinking as an "intentional act" par excellence, distinguishing it clearly from an "intended" act as expressing foremostly the manifestation of will.(TAP, 126)

Person

Question 29 of Part I of the *Summa Theologica* is entitled "The Divine Persons." Article 3 distinguishes between the "origin" of the term "person" and its "objective meaning." St. Thomas will deal with the term "person" as he discusses the Trinity in Questions 27-43. It is in the context of this discussion that his thought on "person" is elucidated.

In Article 3, Question 29, Objection 2, Aquinas quotes Boethius's *On the Two Natures* [of Christ], as Boethius presents the origin of the term "person." Boethius argues that, given its origin, the term could be applied to God only metaphorically.

> The word person seems to be taken from those persons who represented men in comedies and tragedies. For person comes from sounding through (*personando*), since a greater volume of sound is produced through the cavity in the mask. These "persons" [masks] . . . were placed on the face and covered the features before the eyes. (Q. 29, Art. 3, Obj. 2)

At the end of Objection 2, Aquinas says that the word "person" can apply to God only in a metaphorical sense. (Q. 29, Art.

3, Obj. 2) Then in his Reply to Objection 2, Aquinas tells what the "objective meaning" of the term "person" is.

> Although this name *person* may not belong to God as regards the origin of the term, nevertheless it excellently belongs to God in its objective meaning. For as famous men were represented in comedies and tragedies, the name *person* was given to those who held high dignity. Hence, those who held high rank in the Church came to be called *persons*. Thence by some the definition of person is given as *hypostasis* [substance or essential nature of an individual] *distinct by reason of dignity*. And because subsistence in a rational nature is of high dignity, therefore every individual of the rational nature is called a *person*. Now the dignity of the divine nature excels every other dignity; and thus the name *person* pre-eminently belongs to God.(Reply Obj. 2)

Article 1 of Question 29 argues that Boethius's definition of "person" is sufficient: "a person is an individual substance of a rational nature."(Obj. 1)

An analysis of Articles 1 and 2 of Question 29 yields an understanding of this definition of person that is the "objective meaning" of the term. These articles permit an analysis of the terms and phrases 1) person; 2) substance; 3) individual substance; 4) nature; 5) rational nature.

Article 1: 1) Person—In Article 1, Objection 1, Aquinas considers that "person," which signifies "one" or "singular," as a singular, cannot be subject to definition. [Definition is of a genus, kind, type, or set, that is, of what places the "singular" in a class of singulars like itself in one or more ways.] But Aquinas answers his own objection by saying that although this or that singular is not definable, what belongs to the idea of singularity can be defined. Thus Aristotle can give a definition of first substance, which is what Boethius uses in his definition of "person" ("an individual substance, etc.") (Q. 29, Art. 1, Reply Obj. 1)

2) Aquinas considers whether the "substance" of Boethius's definition is "first substance" or "second substance." If "substance" is "first substance," then the word "individual" (in the expression "individual substance") is superfluous because "first substance" is "individual substance." If "substance" is "second substance," the word "individual" is false, the phrase "second substance" then becoming a contradiction in terms, since "second substances" are the *genera* or *species* [class and sub-class]. Such a contradiction would clearly make the definition incorrect. In his reply to this objection, Aquinas says that "in the opinion of some" the term *substance* in the definition of person stands for first substance, which is the hypostasis. He says further that the term "individual" is not superfluous since in the phrase first substance and in the term hypostasis both the idea of universality and that of a part are excluded—mankind is not a hypostasis and neither is a human hand a hypostasis.

Aquinas prefers that "substance" be understood in a general sense, divided into first and second substance. When "individual" is added, it is to be understood as first substance.

Article 2: Aquinas distinguishes "person" from "hypostasis," "subsistence," and "essence." In the first objection he quotes Boethius as saying that "the Greeks called the individual substance of the rational nature by the term hypostasis," and since "hypostasis" signifies for him and for his reader "person," the terms might be thought to be synonymous. In his reply to this objection, he says that while the Greeks took hypostasis in its strict interpretation to mean any individual of the genus substance, in ordinary speech it means the individual of the *rational nature,* since it is the rational nature that is the excellent one.

In summary: person—an individual substance of a rational nature; substance—first substance, what can exist independently, and that in which accidents inhere [Aristotle in the *Categories,* Chapter 4, 25-27, lists substance, which is independent and can "stand alone," and its nine accidents—quantity, quality, relation, place, time, position, state, action, affection]; rational nature—a nature or genus or kind that possesses rationality, an excellence that belongs exclusively to humans.

A person is an individual substance of a rational nature.

In Karol Wojtyla's (Pope John Paul II) *The Acting Person* the discussion of "person" is prepared for by an analysis of the meaning of "experience," viewed phenomenologically and not phenomenally. The latter perspective, the one rejected by Wojtyla, overlooks "the essential unity of the distinctive experiences" in favor of viewing "the unitary nature of experience" as due to its "being composed of a set of sensations or emotions, which are subsequently ordered by the mind."(TAP, 3)

Wojtyla says that when we speak of "the experience of man," we are speaking primarily of man's experience of himself.(TAP, 3) Our knowledge of man is grounded in experience (TAP, 4-5), and an experience is "connected with a range of data which we have as given."(TAP, 9)

In Note 1, Wojtyla says: "In general, for phenomenologists experience means immediate givenness or every cognitive act in which the object itself is given directly—bodily [as *personified* or *incarnate*]...."(TAP, 301)

The fact of "man-acts" is the starting point for Wojtyla. "Acting is a ceaselessly repeated event in the life of every man, so that when we consider the number of living people we obtain innumerable facts and hence an enormous wealth of experience."(TAP, 9)

The objects and facts in surrounding reality are grasped directly in a "sensuous act" but also grasped directly in an "intentional-intellectual act," a cognitive not a sensuous act.(TAP,9) There is a unity in the acts of human cognition.(TAP,10) That in every human experience there is a certain measure of understanding of what is experienced has significance for the study of the person and of action.(TAP,10)

> For our position is that *action serves as a particular moment of apprehending—that is, of experiencing—the person.* (TAP, 10)

Action for Wojtyla is the "particular moment in the apprehension of a person."(TAP, 10) He says that this view defines his approach in the study, *The Acting Person.* (TAP, 10) As he discusses the relation of *person* and *action*, Wojtyla says that ". . . action is not a single event but a process-like sequence of acting; and this corresponds to different agents."(TAP, 11)

> The kind of acting that is an action, however, can be assigned to no other agent than a person. In other words, an action presupposes a person. This has been the standard approach in different fields of learning that have as their object man's acting, and is especially true of ethics, which treats of action that presupposes a person, that is, presupposes man as a person.(TAP, 11)

But Wojtyla proposes in his study to reverse the relation. For him the person is not presupposed and then his action discoursed upon. He will look at the person through the action. The person will be revealed through the action. (TAP, 11)

> Action gives us the best insight into the inherent essence of the person and allows us to understand the person most fully. We experience man as a person, and we are convinced of it because he performs actions. (TAP, 11)

Wojtyla states explicitly that his book is not ethics but an anthropology which must take into account the moral.(TAP, 13) He does not try to prove that man is a person and his acting is "action" but assumes these as given in the experience of man. Each instance of acting contains person and action.(TAP, 15)

Thus the entire study is an "exfoliating" and a "comprehending" of the person.(TAP, 13) Wojtyla sees his study as ". . . possibly the most comprehensive explanation of that reality which is the person."(TAP, 13) Thus he describes the acting person from consciousness (Chapter 1) to intersubjectivity by participation in the community of others (Chapter 7). In his description is included human dynamism (Chapter 2), the person in self-determination (Chapters 3 and 4), the person as integrated in the action (Chapter 5), and the psyche (Chapter 6).

Communion

The "Treatise on the Creation" in Part I of St. Thomas's *Summa Theologica* extends from Question 44 through Question 49. But it is in Question 45, "The Mode of Emanation of Things from the First Principle," that the metaphysical relationship between God and creatures is outlined, and especially in Article 5, "Whether It Belongs to God Alone to Create?" In the "I answer that" section of Article 5, Aquinas says that to create can be the action of God alone.

> For the most universal effects must be reduced to the more universal and prior causes. Now among all effects the most universal is being itself; and hence it must be the proper effect of the first and most universal cause, and that is God.(Q. 45, Art. 5)

Creation is proper to the Blessed Trinity.(Q. 45, Art. 6, I answer that) Moreover, "the trace of the Trinity appears in creatures."(St. Augustine, *On the Trinity*, vi, 10)

St. Thomas discusses "trace." He says that every effect in some degree represents its cause, but diversely. Some effects represent only the causality of the cause, but not its form, as smoke represents fire. "Such a representation is called a *trace:* for a trace shows that someone has passed by but not who it is." (Q. 45, Art. 7, On the contrary)

In each creature are found some things which are necessarily reduced to the Divine Persons as their causes. Each creature subsists in its own being, has a form by which it is part of a species and so has relation to something else outside itself. Since each creature is a created substance, it represents the cause and principle, namely, the Person of the Father, the "principle from no principle." Insofar as each creature has form and species, it represents the Word, just as the form of the thing made by art is from the conception of the craftsman. Each creature is in a relation of order to the will of the Creator, and thus represents the Holy Spirit, who is love [the relation between the Father and the Son].(Q. 45, Art. 7, I answer that)

Augustine says that the trace of the Trinity is found in every

162

creature, according as it is one individual, that which exists (the Father); and according as it is formed by a species, by which it is distinguished (the Son); and according as it has a certain relation of order, by which it agrees (the Holy Spirit).(Q. 45, Art. 7, I answer that)

Earlier in the "I answer that," St. Thomas had referred to Question 27, where he had explained the procession of the Persons of the Trinity. The Son proceeds from the Father as the word of the intellect, and the Holy Ghost proceeds as love of the will. It is in the context of his effort to distinguish the kind of representation which he will call "image" rather than "trace" that St. Thomas points up the dignity of the human creature as over and above all other creatures. All creatures enjoy the representation of the "trace" of the Godhead. Only the human creature enjoys the representation of the "image" of the Godhead.

How is this the case? Every effect represents its cause. Smoke represents fire. The effect, smoke, represents the causality of the cause, fire, but not its form. All creatures represent God. They all show that someone has passed by but not who. Fire generated represents fire generating. The effect, "fire generated," represents the form of its cause, "fire generating." The human creature represents God by the representation called "image." Just as the Son proceeds from the Father as the word of the intellect, and the Holy Spirit as the love of the will, so in rational creatures, possessing intellect and will, there is the representation of the Trinity that is called image, inasmuch as in them is the word conceived and the love proceeding.(Q.45, Art.7, I answer that)

If trace or image of the Trinity, then representation; if representation, then similarity; if similarity, then communion.

In the Third Part of the *Summa Theologica,* St. Thomas treats of the Mystery of the Incarnation (Qq. 1-26), the Blessed Virgin Mary (Qq. 27-43), Our Lord Jesus Christ (Qq. 34-59), and the Sacraments (Qq. 60-90)

In Question 60, "What Is a Sacrament?" St. Thomas calls a sacrament a "sacred secret," since a sacrament has a hidden sanctity. A sacrament also is a sign.(Q. 60, Art. 1, I answer that)

It is a sign of a holy thing so far as it makes men holy.(Q. 60, Art. 2, I answer that) In Article 5 St. Thomas says that in the sacraments two things may be considered: the worship of God and the sanctification of man. The worship of God pertains to man as referred to God, and the sanctification of man pertains to God in reference to man.(Q. 60, Art. 5, I answer that)

This "reference" from man to God and from God to man is also communion.

Question 66, "Of the Sacrament of Baptism," explains that the sacraments effect sanctification and that the sacrament is completed where the sanctification is completed. The water of baptism does not complete the sacrament. Instead a sanctifying instrumental virtue, not permanent but transient, passes from the water into the man who is the true subject of sanctification.(Q. 66, Art. 1, I answer that) Baptism is the beginning of spiritual life.(Q. 66, Art. 1, Reply Obj. 1)

Again, this sanctification unites the baptized to God. It is communion.

In Question 73, "Of the Sacrament of the Eucharist," St. Thomas says that the spiritual life is analogous to the corporeal. Spiritual generation takes place in Baptism; growth in Confirmation; spiritual food and refreshment in the Eucharist.(Q. 73, Art. 1, I answer that)

In Article 4 St. Thomas says that the sacrament of the Eucharist has a threefold significance:

1) with regard to the past it has meaning in that it is commemorative of the Lord's Passion, and so it is called a Sacrifice;

2) with regard to the present it has the meaning of ecclesiastical unity. He quotes John Damascene:

> . . . it is called Communion because we communicate with Christ through it, both because we partake of His flesh and Godhead, and because we communicate with and are united to one another through it. (*On the Orthodox Faith*, iv)

3) with regard to the future it has the meaning of the foreshadowing of the Divine fruition, which will take place in heaven and so it is called *Viaticum* because it provides the way of

winning heaven. In this respect it is also called *Eucharist,* good grace, because *the grace of God is life everlasting* (Romans vi, 23) or because it really contains Christ, who is *full of grace.*

The sacrament of the Eucharist is then a communion with the Lord's Passion, communion with Christ and with all believers, and a communion with life everlasting insofar as it is a provision for heaven.

Part Four, "Participation," of Wojtyla's *The Acting Person,* presents Chapter Seven, "Intersubjectivity by Participation." Section 3, "A More Detailed Definition of 'Participation,'" refers to the notion of participation as conceived in traditional philosophy, that is, not simply taking part with others in one thing or another, but participation in its philosophical and theological sense—the basis of man's place in interaction.(TAP, 268)

Wojtyla notes that traditionally participation was connected with the idea of nature; for him, the person's transcendence in the action, when the action is being performed together with others, is the focus. Wojtyla wants to save the freedom of the person, and he judges that freedom saved in the personalistic emphasis of participation. Social exchange, working together, various forms of community—no one of these can destroy the transcendence of the person in action.(TAP, 268-69)

Section 4, "Individualism and Anti-Individualism," points to two extremes, both of which inhibit participation understood as both taking part with others and yet transcending the taking part in such a way as not to be "swallowed up" by community. The first extreme is individualism and the second is totalism. Wojtyla sees both systems, individualism and totalism (or anti-individualism), as impersonalistic or antipersonalistic.(TAP, 271-75)

In these sections of Chapter Seven and in all of the other sections it is clear that Wojtyla is not attempting a theological study of the idea of participation, nor of communion. This work is a philosophical anthropology and as such leaves the depth of the author's theological understanding to other writings of his.

"Intersubjectivity by Participation" does provide, however, a full preamble to theological reflection on the human being and communion. Section 10, the last before the "Postscript," is entitled "The Commandment of Love."

In Section 9 Wojtyla has dealt with the two interrelated systems of reference—fellow member and neighbor. Now in Section 10 he identifies the neighbor as the fundamental system of reference. Because of the evangelical commandment of love, says Wojtyla, there is "... a sort of transcendence of being a neighbor with regard to being a member of a community." Nevertheless, man as a member of community may not limit himself as neighbor, nor may man as neighbor limit himself as member of a community. The two systems of reference are interrelated.(TAP, 292-99)

Just as the person's transcendence in his action with others saves his freedom, saves him from conditioning, from the determinism of pure "nature," so the neighbor's priority over "member of community" saves both the imperative laid on him to love his neighbor as himself and his neighbor's imperative to do the same.

Transcendence

In Aquinas the term is "transcendentals," the more modern terms "transcendence," "transcendent," "transcend" deriving more from German philosophy or from the more literary leanings of British, American, and other writers influenced by the philosophers.

An Introduction to the Metaphysics of St. Thomas Aquinas is composed of texts selected and translated by James F. Anderson from various writings of Aquinas.[4] The texts on the transcendentals are from *On Truth*, I, 1.

What the intellect first conceives is being. The intellect conceives being first because being is the most intelligible (most evident to the mind) object available to the intellect. To being the intellect reduces all its other conceptions. All these other conceptions have to be arrived at by addition to being.(IMSTA, 44)

Aquinas held that the transcendentals—one, true, good, beautiful—go beyond the categories of being that Aristotle named (substance, and the nine accidents) and apply to everything. All that has being is one, true, good, beautiful.

All that exists is one—undivided.(IMSTA, 49) All that exists is true—being [what is] and intellect [the mind knowing] correspond to one another.(IMSTA,61) All that exists is good—everything that is tends toward a perfection, a fulfillment, a rest.(IMSTA, 83) All that exists is beautiful—what is exists as a form and as such shares in the divine splendor; each thing has its own splendor of form or *claritas*.(IMSTA, 92)

Wojtyla in *The Acting Person* uses the term "transcendence" to refer to the manner in which the person acts. It is in order to assert the freedom and the spirituality of man that Wojtyla chooses to use the term "transcendence." He writes:

> The one who acts *is* the person and asserts himself as "somebody"; and at the same time he even more vividly and completely demonstrates in his acting, in the action, why he deserves to be regarded as "somebody." Indeed, he shows himself as having the special ability and power of self-governance which allows him to have the experience of himself as a free being. Freedom is expressed by efficacy and efficacy leads to responsibility, which in turn reveals the dependence of freedom on truth; but this relation of freedom to truth constitutes the real significance of the conscience as the decisive factor for the transcendence of the person in his actions.(TAP, 180)

To "transcend" is to "go beyond," "to cut across," whether it is going beyond what is perceptible to the senses, cutting across the merely material, or going beyond and cutting across the sense of being determined or controlled by nature or environment, or going beyond, cutting across one's own supposed needs, one's cultivated desires. In all cases, transcendence is rooted in the human connection with the Divine, and flowers in the connection between human beings.

Mercy

In Part II-II, *Summa Theologica*, Question 30, St. Thomas treats "Of Mercy." He asks four questions: 1) Whether evil is properly the motive of mercy? 2) Whether the reason for taking pity is a defect in the person who pities? 3) Whether mercy is a virtue? 4) Whether it is the greatest of virtues?

To the first, St. Thomas answers "yes"; to the second, "yes"; to the third, "yes"; and to the fourth, "no."

It is the second question, especially with St. Thomas's qualification on the affirmative answer, and also the fourth question that challenge the most interest. It is not so hard to see that one may feel mercy, defined as pity, for the evils one encounters, nor is it difficult to see that mercy is a virtue. But to understand how mercy, or taking pity, is a defect in the one extending the mercy or pity and yet is an attribute of God requires a closer look. Also, to grasp why mercy is not the greatest of virtues is important for those who already know that it is charity that receives this highest status.

Mercy in God is no defect. "God takes pity on us through love alone, in as much as He loves us as belonging to Him."(Q. 30, Art. 2, Reply Obj. 1) In all others, pity is a kind of sorrow, and a defect is a reason of sorrow.(Q. 30, Art. 2, On the contrary)

Charity is the greatest of the virtues.(Q. 30, Art. 4, On the contrary) But a virtue may be greatest in two ways: in itself and in comparison with its subject. In itself mercy is the greatest. It pertains to mercy to be bountiful to others; thus mercy is proper to God, who has the wherewithal *par excellence* to succor all others. With regard to its subject, mercy is not the greatest unless the subject is the greatest. If anyone is above me, it is better for me to be united to him than to think that I can succor him; I cannot. Thus it is better for me if I am beneath him to be united by charity. I am certainly beneath God. Thus in that regard, charity is the greatest.(Q. 30, Art. 4, I answer that)

Yet of the virtues which relate to my neighbor, mercy is the greatest. By mercy we supply for defects of our neighbor.(Q. 30, Art. 4, I answer that)

Finally, with regard to external works, the sum total of the Christian religion consists in mercy. But the inward love of charity, by which we are united to God, stands above both love and mercy for our neighbor.(Q. 30, Art. 4, Reply Obj. 2)

> Charity likens us to God by uniting us to Him in the bond of love: wherefore it surpasses mercy, which likens us to God as regards similarity of works. (Q. 30, Art. 4, Reply Obj. 3)

Notes

1. This definition of "intention" is from the Glossary, St. Thomas Aquinas, *Summa Theologiae*, 1a-2ae, Questions 18-21, ed. Thomas Gilby, O.P., "Principles of Morality," Volume XVIII, Latin text and English translation (London: Blackfriars with Eyre and Spottiswoode; New York: McGraw-Hill Book Company, 1966) 194.

2. Aquinas, Thomas, *Summa Theologica,* Westminster, Maryland, 1981. Citations are by Part, Question, Article, Objection, On the contrary, I answer that, and Reply to objection.

3. Wojtyla, Karol (Pope John Paul II), *The Acting Person,* 125. All further references to this work are cited in the text as TAP.

4. *Introduction to the Metaphysics of St. Thomas Aquinas,* texts selected and translated by James F. Anderson (Chicago: Henry Regnery Company, Gateway Edition, 1969). All references to this work are cited in the text as IMSTA.

Selected Bibliography

The books that should be named, given the intentions of *Thinkers through Time,* are under the Suggested Readings or Works By at the end of chapters. The works listed here are not included in those bibliographies.

Bernasconi, Robert and Simon Critchley, eds. *Re-Reading Levinas.* Bloomington and Indianapolis: Indiana University Press, 1991.

Burkhardt, Hans and Barry Smith, eds. *Handbook of Metaphysics and Ontoloqy.* Munich and Philadelphia: Philosophia Verlag, 1991.

Collinson, Diané. *Fifty Major Philosophers.* New York: Croom Helm, 1987.

Finnis, John. *Natural Law and Natural Rights.* Oxford: Clarendon Press, 1980.

Gadamer, Hans-Georg. *The Idea of the Good in Platonic-Aristotelian Philosophy.* Trans. P.Christopher Smith. New Haven: Yale University Press, 1986.

Griswold, Charles L., ed. *Platonic Writings, Platonic Readings.* New York: Routledge, Chapman & Hall, Inc., 1988.

Guthrie, W.K.C. *The Sophists.* New York: Cambridge University Press, 1971.

Johnson, Oliver A. *Ethics: Selections from Classical and Contemporary Writers,* Fifth Edition. New York: Holt, Rinehart and Winston, 1984.

Kaufmann, Walter. *Existentialism from Dostoevsky to Sartre.* New York: New American Library, 1975.

Kenny, Anthony. *Aquinas.* Past Masters Series, ed. Keith Thomas. New York: Hill and Wang, 1980.

Kirk, G.S. and J.E. Raven. *The Presocratic Philosophers.* New York: Cambridge University Press, 1957.

MacIntyre, Alasdair. *Whose Justice? Which Rationality?* Notre Dame, Indiana: University of Notre Dame Press, 1988.

——————. *Three Rival Versions of Moral Enquiry.* Notre Dame, Indiana: University of Notre Dame Press, 1990.

Runes, Dagobert D., ed. *Dictionary of Philosophy.* Savage, Maryland: Littlefield, Adams, 1983.

Silverman, Hugh J., ed. *Continental Philosophy I: Philosophy and Non-Philosophy Since Merleau-Ponty.* New York: Routledge, Chapman and Hall, Inc., 1988.

Simon, Yves R. *An Introduction to Metaphysics of Knowledge.* Trans. Vukan Kuic and Richard J. Thompson. New York: Fordham University Press, 1990.

Vlastos, Gregory, ed. *Plato I: Metaphysics and Epistemology.* Notre Dame, Indiana: University of Notre Dame Press, 1978.

INDEX

Abraham 119
Achilles 50
Accountability 85-86
Acting Person, The (Wojtyla) 3, 94n., 155, 160, 169n.
Albert the Great, St. 39
Alexander the Great 25
Anderson, James F. 3, 166
Antigone 2, 14ff., 35
Aquinas, St. Thomas 2, 39ff., 52-53n., works of 56, 145ff., 151ff., 169n.
Aristotle 2, 7, 25ff., 35, 36n., works by 38, 42, 45
Athens 7, 19, 25, 121
Augustine, St. 149

Being, idea of 42, loss of sense of 100, 102-103, participation in 104
Bible 118
Boethius 148-149, 157-158
Buddhism 137, 140

Caesar, Julius 47
Callicles 212n.
Camus Albert 2, 120ff.
Categorical imperative 76-77, 78
Catholic faith 82-83, 97, 137

Charity 165
Choragos 31
Christ 92, 128ff.
Christianity 89, 123, 137-138
Church 111
City of God, The (Augustine) 149
Cleopatra 50
Collected Philosophical Papers (Levinas) 2, 125
Cologne 39
Communion, theme of, 2, 97ff., 110, 151, 162ff.
Consolation of Philosophy (Boethius) 148
Created rational being 59 60, 65, 79, 162
Creation 162
Creon 14ff., 31ff.
Critique of Practical Reason (Kant) 2, 58ff.
Critique of Pure Reason (Kant) 57

Dante 2, 48ff.
Delphi, Oracle of 31, 33
Descartes, René 53
Dido 50
Dion 7
Dionysius 7

Dives in Misericordia (John Paul II) 128
Divine Comedy, The (Dante) 44ff., 54-55
Dominicans 39
Duty 58, 60, 62, 65, 77

Egypt 7
Einstein, Albert 90
Ekdal 65ff.
Elenchos (elenctic argument) 7-8, 20-21n.
Endo, Shusaku 2, 137ff.
Eteocles 14, 16
Ethics 1, 83, 85, of "the other" 115ff., 123, 146
Eucken, Rudolf 82
Eurydice 15, 16
Evil, nature of 43
Existentialism 111n., 112n.
Existentialists 97

Fidelity 99
Fortitude 147, 168-169
Foundations of the Metaphysics of Morals (Kant) 77
Function(s) 101-102

Geneva 82
Germany 57
God 49-50, 52, 54-55n., 59-60, 63, 90, 100, 110-111, idea of 119, 120, 123, 124n., rich in mercy 128, 150, as Trinity 162-164, 168-169
Good, idea of 42, nature of 43, to be done 46, desire for 115, 118, 123, of human acts 152-153, 154
Good Samaritan 132
Gospel 62-63
Guinivere 49

Haemon 15, 16
Hamilton, Edith 2ln.
Happiness, theme of, 2, 25ff., virtuous activity of the soul 30, and justice, 145ff., 147ff.
Happy man, the 31
Heidegger, Martin 97, 115
Homer 10
Hope 99
Hubris 16
Husserl, Edmund 82, 115

Ibsen, Henrik 2, 65ff.
Incentives 63-64
Inferno (Dante) 2, 48ff., 54-55n.
Infinite, the 119-120
Intention, theme of 2, 57, 58ff, 79, 87, 151, 153-154, distingished from intent 156
Introduction to the Metphysics of St. Thomas Aquinas (Anderson) 3, 166
Isaac 119
Isidore, St. 45
Ismene 14, 35

Jagiellonian University 127
Jacob 119
Jaspers, Karl 97
Jena, University of 82
Jeweler's Shop, The (Wojtyla) 2, 104ff.
Jocasta 14, 31ff.
John the Baptist 130
Justice, theme of 2, 7ff., as virtue 13, 145, specific of man 14, in *Antigone,* 14, profitable 17, 20, and happiness 145ff., definition of 146

Kakure (Japanese descendants of Christian converts) 137, 139-140

Kant, Immanuel 2, 21n., 53n.,
   57ff., 77ff., works of 80-81
Konigsberg 57
Knutzen, Martin 57
Krakow 127, 128

Lancelot 49
Laios 31,33
Levinas, Emmanuel 1, 21n, 53n.,
   115ff., works of 125-126
Lithuania 115
London 121
Luciani, Albino. See Pope John
   Paul I
Lyons, Council of 39

MacIntyre, Alasdair 20n., 54n.
Marcel, Gabriel 2, 97ff., works by
   114
Mary, as mother of mercy 136,
   140, 163
Marseilles 121
Maturity 88, 93
Merope 33-34
Mercy, theme of 2, 127ff., mother
   of 136, 151, 168-169
Messiah 130
Metaphysics 42, 98
Metaphysics (Aristotle) 42
Milan 121
Mind, soundness of 83-84, 93
Minos 50
Monte Cassino 39
Moral fanaticism 58, 62-63, 64
Moral law 60-61, 65, 79
Morality 1, theme of 2, 39,
   reasonableness of 40, 48, first
   principles of 42, habit of 44
"Mothers" (Endo) 2, 136ff.
Mother of Sorrows 140
Munich 82

Mystery 100, 112n., of the Father
   128, of election 134

Naples, University of 39
Natural Law 39ff., first principle
   of 42, 51, precepts of 40-43,
   universality of 45,
   unchangeableness of 47, in the
   heart 47-48
Nazism 121
Nicomachean Ethics (Aristotle) 2,
   25, 35, 36n., 148

Ockham, William of 52-53n.
Oedipus Rex (Sophocles) 2, 31ff.,
   37n.
Old Testament 118, 132-133
On the Mercy of God (Pope John
   Paul II) 3
Oran 120-121

"Paolo and Francesca" (Dante)
   48ff.
Paradiso (Dante) 50, 54n.
Paris 50, 97
Paris, University of 39
Participation 65ff.
Passivity 116
Percy, Walker 2, 90ff.
Person, theme of 2, as primary
   82ff., 151, 157-160, definition of
   158-160
Personal values 83ff.
Physics (Aristotle) 45
Plague, The (Camus) 2, 120ff.
Plato, 1, 3. 7ff., 17n., 22n , works
   by 23-24, 26
Platonic ideas 26
Poetics (Aristotle) 25
Poland 127
Polemarchus 8ff., 13, 16

Polybus 33
Polynices 14ff.
Pope Paul VI 128
Pope John Paul I 128
Pope John Paul II 2, 3, 94n., 96n.,
  104ff., 113n., 127ff., 141n.,
  151ff., 155ff., 160ff., 169n.
Precepts 40-43
Prodigal Son 134-135
Prussia 57
Purgatorio (Dante) 50, 54-55n.

Reason, practical 42, 45
Reason, speculative 42, 45
Republic, The (Plato) 2, 7, 8, 14, 17,
  20, 23n.
Responsihility 85-86, 116, 123
Rome 127

Sacrament 163-164
Sanctity 98
Sartre, Jean-Paul 97
Scotland 57
Second Coming, The (Percy) 2, 90ff
.
Self-evident propositions 41
Semiramis 50
Scheler, Max 1, 2, 82ff., 99n.,
  works of 96
Scripture 118, 132-133
Shinto 137
Sicily 7
Simonides 8, 10
Socrates 7, 8ff., 17, 20n.
Sophists 19n.
Sophocles 2, 3, 14ff., 31ff., 37n.
Sorbonne 97, 115
Soul 84-85, 89
Sparta 7
Sphinx 31
Stagira 25

Stockholm 97
Strasburg, University of 115
Subjectivity 116-117
Summa Theologica (St. Thomas) 2,
  3, 39ff., 52n., 145, 147, 151ff.,
  157, 162, 169
Sympathy 122
Syracuse 7

Teiresias 15, 31ff.
Temperance 147, 168-169
Thebes 14, 31
Theft, morality of 47
Thrasymachus 8, 11ff., 19n., 20
Tokyo 136
Transcendence, theme of, 2, 119-
  120, 122-123, 124n., 151, 166-167
Tristan 50

Understanding condition of
  being a person, 83

Virgil 49-50
Virtue 13, 27-28, as pleasant 29,
  activity of the soul 30, natural
  ness of 44-45, 64, justice as
  habit and virtue 145, temper
  ance and fortitude 147, 168-169
Vlastos, Gregory 17ff., comments
  on 18-19
Vulnerability 117

Werle, Gregers 65ff.
Wild Duck, The (Ibsen) 2, 65ff., 80
Wojtyla, Karol. See Pope John
  Paul II

About the Author

Sister Mary Bernard Curran was born in Yonkers, New York, and later moved to Hampton, Virginia. She joined the Dominican Sisters of the St. Cecilia Congregation, Nashville, Tennessee. She received the B.A. degree in English from Peabody College of Vanderbilt University, Nashville, and the M.A. degree in English from De Paul University, Chicago. She studied philosophy at The Catholic University of America, Washington, D.C., where she received the Ph.L. She did further studies in philosophy at Vanderbilt in Nashville and at Memphis State University. She has taught at Aquinas College in Nashville and is presently residing in Memphis.